Classics of Christian Inspiration

LOVE NEVER FAILETH

Love vaunteth not itself,
is not puffed up;
doth not behave itself unseemly;
seeketh not her own,
is not easily provoked,
thinketh no evil . . .
Love never faileth.

I CORINTHIANS 13

Love Never Faileth

❧

EKNATH EASWARAN

ON SAINT FRANCIS,

SAINT PAUL,

SAINT AUGUSTINE &

MOTHER TERESA

❧

With Introductions by Carol Lee Flinders

❧

NILGIRI PRESS

Second edition, first printing August 1996

The Blue Mountain Center of Meditation, founded in
Berkeley, California, in 1961 by Eknath Easwaran,
publishes books on how to lead the spiritual life
in the home and the community.
For information please write to
Nilgiri Press, Box 256, Tomales, California 94971

Printed on recycled, permanent paper.
The paper used in this publication meets the minimum requirements of American
National Standard for Information Services - Permanence of Paper for Printed
Library Materials, ANSI Z39.48—1984

Library of Congress Cataloging in Publication Data:
Easwaran, Eknath.
Love Never Faileth / Eknath Easwaran on Saint Francis, Saint Paul, Saint
Augustine & Mother Teresa with introductions by Carol Lee Flinders. — 2nd ed.
p. cm. — (Classics of Christian inspiration series)
Includes bibliographical references and index.
ISBN 0—915132—90—7 (alk. paper). —
ISBN 0—915132—89—3 (pbk. : alk. paper)
1. Spiritual life. 2. Spiritual life — Christianity. I. Title.
BL624.E165 1996
282'.092'2 — dc20   [B]   96—25217   CIP

Table of Contents

Introduction by Carol Lee Flinders

It happened to Augustine, and it happened to Francis of Assisi – in a garden, to the one; to the other, in a dilapidated chapel. To Paul it happened while he was Saul the tentmaker, on the road to Damascus, engulfing him in a light so bright he saw nothing for three days afterward. And to Teresa, a Sister of Loreto, it happened as she sat on a train headed for Darjeeling – happened so simply and quietly there's almost nothing to tell.

"God spoke to me," they say, and their lives compel our belief. Struck down by love, charged then to live it, they are no longer Augustine or Francis or Teresa but "Saint" or "Blessed" or, to millions of God's homeless and hungry children, just "Mother." No longer a finite human being but a force, barely contained in flesh and bone. "Not I, not I, but Christ liveth in me."

The pattern is never exactly the same twice. With Paul, for instance, there seems to have been a complete and radical reversal: Saul of Tarsus gone in a flash; Paul, "the new man," there in his stead, and no one more surprised than he. With Mother Teresa, on the other hand, there is no sudden transformation, but a simple, gradual unfolding – one long, pure, unflinching acquiescence. (Asked for "legends" about Mother Teresa as a young nun, one of her earliest associates protests, "But there are no legends about her. Mother Teresa is completely normal.") These are extremes. Set down all similar "cases" and they fall somewhere between, but always there seems to be that "still, small voice," coming just when it's needed most.

One envies them so, these great souls who know themselves "called," know without a doubt that what they are doing has divine sanction and even complicity. It is hard not to think of them as almost superhuman. Setting them apart as "Saint Thus and Such" only makes matters worse.

In fact, Easwaran's purpose in looking at the lives and words of these individuals is not to set them apart from the rest of us, but to connect us to them, directly and vitally, in the manner of a physician readying a patient for a transfusion. Individuals like Bernard of Clairvaux, Catherine of Siena, George Fox, John Woolman, Saint Vincent de Paul, and Teresa of Avila have elevated the period of history in which they lived, and they continue to inspire even now. Yet there is nothing any of them did, Easwaran would insist, that isn't within the reach of every human being.

Years ago, when Easwaran was giving the nightly classes in meditation with which he began his work in this country, he used to enjoy describing his first and only trip to Yosemite National Park. It gave him a chance to tease without mercy the friend who'd taken him there — this had been his first exposure to the American passion for the Right Equipment, the Perfect Campsite, the Well-Built Fire. But he had a point to make too.

As day faded into night, he recalled, the din on the valley floor was intolerable. Transistor radios, car engines, parents and children calling out to one another — you might as well have stayed in downtown Berkeley. By ten o'clock, though, the last radio was turned off and the last exuberant child bedded down. Silence fell across the campground. And in the silence, audible at last, he heard the faint, murmuring music of a stream that passed just ten feet from his tent. He hadn't even known it was there.

Just so, he tells us, the "still, small voice" of God murmurs within every one of us all the time — advising us, consoling and strengthening us — an endless wellspring of wisdom and inspiration. The only reason we don't hear it as clearly as Francis or Augustine did is that we've allowed too many other noises to drown it out: the raucous voice of self-will, the clamor of selfish desire, the shrill tones of anxiety and fear. Silence them one by one, through meditation and the allied disciplines, and Francis's experience at San Damiano or Augustine's in his garden will no longer seem like a fairy tale at all.

Hearing the stream is one thing: following it to the source, the clear, pure spring itself, is another. Looking at the lives of the great men and women of God, one gathers that there is a reciprocity between prayer, or meditation, and action — a powerful mandate to live out what is heard in the depths of consciousness, and a deepening of the inner life each time you do. Small tasks lead outward into larger ones, the ante rising with each willing response, as the individual becomes a more and more perfect instrument of the divine will.

It is in the final stages of this process, says Easwaran, that you make an endlessly astonishing discovery. When the senses have been brought under control, when the mind is stilled and self-will extinguished and the voice you've heard just barely, just for seconds, is finally distinct — loud and clear at long last — you realize that it is your own. Your innermost self is inseparable from the Lord.

Each ordinary one of us, then, conceals an immense power for good. That power, the capacity for "love in

Introduction by Carol Lee Flinders

The loves and writings of the great spiritual figures are so wonderfully diverse that for almost all of us one or another speaks with special force. Saint Augustine, for instance, has long been a special favorite of people with an intellectual bent — those who have pressed the rational mind to its limits and said finally, "No, no, there has to be more than this." To those with no intellectual pretensions whatsoever, figures like Rose of Lima or Joseph of Cupertino are particularly dear.

Francis of Assisi, though, belongs to everyone. He is the saint with whom just about everybody believes they have a special, private understanding.

It's not immediately clear why. If you really look at what he was doing and how he lived — the ashes he would scatter across a dinner that looked a little too good, the single rough garment he wore, tied at the waist with a rope, the crude thrown-together huts where he and his Brothers spent long, prayerful, icy-cold winter nights — if you look at it squarely, nothing could be more off-putting. Not that it was peculiar — Francis only did what people have always done when they yearn to loose spirit from flesh. But it doesn't typically endear them to others.

Nor does he seem to have possessed other qualities that

usually inspire a following. Crude as his assessment was, considering that he himself was a Friar, Brother Masseo can probably be forgiven for blurting out one day, "Why after you? Why after you?" — adding in explanation, "You are not beautiful to look upon; you are not a man of great knowledge; you are not of noble birth. Why, then, does all the world follow you?"

Francis sought, in the words of his own Rule, "to follow the teaching and the footsteps of our Lord Jesus Christ," which for him meant a life of intense and prayerful austerity. He was not the first man or woman to do so. What sets him apart, though, what keeps his memory warm and alive all over the world today and makes him perhaps the most beloved of saints, is that he made it look like fun.

Compared to the thousand-odd manuscripts that remained in Augustine's library at Hippo, we have almost nothing written by Francis. A last testament, a couple of poems, a few letters — no scriptural commentary, no theological treatise. Francis was mortally suspicious of the world of letters. He chose instead to teach by and through his own actions. So it is most appropriate that the real memorial to the Little Man of Assisi is his life — a life chronicled as lovingly and attentively as almost none has been before the modern period: by Thomas of Celano, by Saint Bonaventura, by his own Brother Leo, and by many, many others. At least once in a generation, someone is inspired to retell his story: writers as diverse as Nikos Kazantzakis and G. K. Chesterton, filmmakers as dissimilar as Roberto Rossellini and Franco Zefferelli. And always, shining through even the most poignant or downright harrowing episodes, there is that joy — exceeding joy — just barely subdued.

"Why after you?" There was no questioning "why"

when Francis was the leader of Assisi's young men about town. He was charming, witty, generous, and musical — a troubadour who composed love songs, the life, soul, and pocketbook of every party. A serious illness cut across all this when he was twenty-two, plunging him during his recovery into a newly introspective mood. After the second of two failed attempts to take up a life of soldiering, he entered a period of even deeper soul-searching.

He would spend his days now in the ruined church of San Damiano outside Assisi, and it was on one of those days that he heard a voice, coming, he thought, from the crucifix: "Go hence, now, Francis, and build up my church, for it is nearly falling down." His response was literal and immediate — and pivotal. Within a few months, he had left forever the home he grew up in and had given himself over entirely to his new calling.

Over the next two years, Francis rebuilt three churches that had fallen into bad disrepair. But this was only the beginning. For he soon realized that his real mission was to infuse vitality and strength into the Church itself — and this he did, in every way conceivable.

Francis's work began with the founding of the Friars Minor, the "Little Brothers" of Christ, who would go out into the world preaching and extending spiritual friendship everywhere. Not long after came the order founded by — and named after — his first woman disciple, Clare. To the Poor Clares there still clings the fragrance of a romance so pure and perfect as to have made the entire Courtly Love tradition look vulgar in comparison. No less important, though, was the Third Order, which adapted the Franciscan pattern for men and women, married or single, whose calling was not monastic. They were to care for the sick and give to the poor, detaching themselves from whatever wealth they might possess and using it as

God's stewards. Pledged to make peace with their enemies, to restore ill-gotten gains, never to bear arms, and never to accept public honors, members of the Order were a strong force for peace in the violent and unstable social structure of the thirteenth century.

Francis's real contribution, though, goes far beyond the institutional. So profound was his devotion that it awakened a great depth of feeling in others: he quite literally taught the people of his region, and generations to come, how to worship.

There was Christmas, three years before Francis would pass away, when he arranged that in the little town of Greccio a replica of the stable at Bethlehem should be constructed, complete with donkey, ox, and manger. Bearing candles and torches, all the men and women of the region came together. "The night was lighted up like the day, and it delighted men and beasts. . . . The woods rang with the voices of the crowd and the rocks made answer to their jubilation." The mystery of the Incarnation came to life anew for everyone there. "The saint of God stood before the manger, uttering sighs, overcome with love. . . ." The mass was celebrated, Francis sang the Gospel, and then he preached "charming words concerning the nativity of the poor King and the little town of Bethlehem." To one man in particular there came a wonderful vision. "He saw a child lying in the manger lifeless, and he saw Francis go and rouse the child, as from a deep sleep. . . ." The symbolic meaning was lost on no one.

Francis sought to identify himself so completely with Christ that His love would reenter the world through His servant. That could only mean one thing to him, which was to seek nothing for himself and offer everything to God. To the suffering he had always imposed upon himself — the privation of every creature comfort — there came to be added the enormous sorrow of seeing his own Order torn apart by dissension and finding himself unable to restore it to unity. Finally, in seclusion on the mountain La Verna, whose great cracks and fissures were believed to have opened up at the moment when Christ was crucified, he lifted his heart to God in perfect abandonment of self — and he was answered. From that time forth, Francis would bear on his hands and feet, and in his side, the unremittingly painful marks of Christ's own anguish.

⌦

I have said "he made it look like fun," and that must seem flippant by now. But in fact this was the enormous paradox of Francis's life. He wedded himself joyously to poverty, called her his bride, his Lady, and played the exuberant bridegroom to the hilt. He was always the troubadour, the "*jongleur de Dieu,*" who taught that good cheer is not just a kindness to all around, but one of the three ways to obtain peace (obedience and prayer being the other two). "Rejoice always," he would say, because it's when the soul is dark and troubled, sullen and lonely, that it turns to the world to seek comfort. "Spiritual joy arises from purity of heart and perseverance in prayer." Ebullience, therefore, and a marvelous sense of good theater are the hallmarks of Francis's life and his way of teaching.

The lives of saints are shot through, for instance, with accounts of Lust Overcome. To call it merely "lust" doesn't really say it, of course — doesn't imply the quieter yet often more tenacious yearnings for home, children, and partner that help make the monastic calling so arduous. The lone monk or nun keeps grim vigil night after night in a narrow cell while the demons of the mind itself dance around them, and eventually — archetypally, anyway — those demons are banished. Nowhere, though, do we read that any of them except Francis burst right out of that cell — a hut in his case — into the snow outside, rolled in it bared to the waist, and then piled it up into *seven* (that's right, seven) snow people.

"Here they are, Francis," he exulted. "Here is your family. The big one over there is your wife. Those are your children, and there are your two servants."

"But Francis," he chided himself. "They're cold. Have you nothing to put on them? If you do not, then aren't you glad you have only your God to serve?"

In fact, Francis never abandoned his desire for a family. He simply expanded the normal idea of what a family is until it embraced all women, all children, and all men — all animals and birds and even insects. The sun and moon he took as siblings and finally even the very elements: "Sister Water, which is very useful and humble and precious and chaste"; "Brother Fire . . . beautiful, jocund, robust, and strong."

It's as if, when he ran out of that hut, he brought the whole Western spiritual tradition with him and showed us once and for all that nothing is excluded from the spiritual life: that all forms of love are perfectly realized by the man or woman who leaves selfish desire behind.

The longer you study his life, the more obvious are the parallels with other saints. And yet there's no one like him, and that's the beauty of it. G. K. Chesterton, one of his most hopelessly smitten biographers, pointed out that you could never anticipate what Francis would do or say in a given situation. But once he had done it or said it, all you could say was "Ah, how like him!"

Did Brother Masseo's challenge go unanswered, then? Did Francis just smile enigmatically and go on his way?

No, the chroniclers tell us. Beaming with delight (months at a time would probably pass without his getting such an opportunity to forbear) he raised his eyes to heaven and remained for a time absorbed in God. Then he knelt down and gave thanks, and when he turned at last to his Brother, said:

"Would you know why they follow after me? Because the eyes of the Most High God have not seen anywhere among the sinners anyone more vile, or more imperfect, or a greater sinner than I. . . . He has elected me to confound the nobility, the majesty, the right, the beauty, and the wisdom of the world, in order to make it known that every virtue and every good thing comes from Him and not from the creature."

✥

From the very beginnings of Easwaran's work in this country, Saint Francis has been a cherished presence. Do we balk at the idea of bringing the body and senses under some measure of control? There is Francis, characterizing his own body as "Brother Ass." "He needs you to feed him," Easwaran elaborates, "and to feed him only so much as he needs – to shelter him, and give him rest when he's tired, and be kind to him in every way, a true friend. But make no mistake – you are the rider, not he!"

Do the finer points of "putting others first" keep eluding us? Lessons in *caritas* leap out from every page of Francis's life, like the night when a Brother cried out in his sleep, "Brothers! I die of hunger!" Swift was Francis's response – but exquisitely tactful. All the Brothers were awakened; all were called to the low table, and all were commanded to break bread together, while Francis spoke tenderly of the danger of excessive mortifications. The friar who had cried out was never named.

There may be no more perfect distillation of all that Francis lived for than the simple prayer Easwaran invariably suggests for use in meditation, which begins, "Lord, make me an instrument of thy peace. . . ."

Lord, make me an instrument of thy peace.
Where there is hatred, let me sow love;
Where there is injury, pardon;
Where there is doubt, faith;
Where there is despair, hope;
Where there is darkness, light;
Where there is sadness, joy.

O divine Master, grant that I may not so much seek
To be consoled as to console,
To be understood as to understand,
To be loved as to love:
For it is in giving that we receive,
It is in pardoning that we are pardoned,
It is in dying to self that we are born to eternal life.

Make Me an Instrument

[1]

When I first came to this country, in 1959, I looked hard for a suitable meditation passage for the West. In this Prayer of Saint Francis I found the perfect answer. During all these years I have been recommending it to everyone because, as you can see, it is a very rare thing: an attempt to reverse almost all the ordinary tendencies we find in human nature. It gives us a blueprint for making our life a blessing for everyone.

In this profoundest of prayers, Saint Francis confides in us how the son of Pietro di Bernardone was transformed into a son of God. We too can aspire to such a transformation by making his Prayer an integral part of our consciousness. This cannot be done through reading or discussion, which take place only on the surface level of consciousness. It can only be done by regular, systematic meditation. If we meditate on Saint Francis's words diligently and with enthusiasm every morning, the marvelous transformation that Francis worked in himself will gradually be effected in us too.

This word "meditation" means many different things to different people. It has been applied to dancing and to listening to music and even to letting the mind wander, which is just the opposite of meditation. I want to explain right from the outset that when I talk about meditation, I mean only one thing: systematically training the mind to focus completely on a lofty ideal until that ideal absorbs our every faculty and passion. In the West this focusing of the mind is often called "interior prayer" or "contemplation," the word "meditation" being used for a kind of disciplined reflection on a single religious theme (such as the Passion) and its significance. But whatever term is used, the practice I am referring to is universal. It has been described in every major spiritual tradition. If you look at the writings of early figures of Christianity like the Desert Fathers, I think you will agree that they would immediately recognize the method I myself follow and teach.

For those who are not familiar with this method, a brief summary will clarify the references to meditation I make throughout the rest of this book.

Instructions in Meditation

Begin by devoting half an hour every morning as early as convenient to the practice of meditation. If you want to meditate more, have half an hour in the evening also, but do not meditate longer than half an hour at a time.

If you do not have a meditation room in your home, a special corner set aside for that purpose will do. Whichever you choose, your meditation place should be quiet. Keep it simple and attractive with a few religious pictures if they appeal to you.

Sit in a straight-backed chair – one with arms – or cross-legged on the floor, with spinal column erect and eyes gently closed. As your concentration deepens, you may begin to relax and fall asleep. If so, draw yourself up and move away from your back support so that you can keep spine, neck, and head in a straight line.

To meditate on the Prayer of Saint Francis, you will need to know the words by heart. (Until you learn them, you can begin with a passage from Scripture that you already know, such as the Lord's Prayer or the Twenty-third Psalm.) Go through the words in your mind as slowly as you can, letting each word drop singly into your consciousness like a jewel. Do not follow any association of ideas, but keep to the words of the Prayer. If you are giving them your full attention, you do not have to turn them over in your mind; the meaning cannot help sinking in.

Similarly, when distractions come, do not resist them; that way they will seize your attention. Instead, simply try to give more and more attention to the words of the Prayer.

It is said that once Saint Francis carved a small cup and was so pleased with his handiwork that his eyes kept wandering back to it even during prayer. When suddenly he realized that the cup was taking his thoughts away from God, he picked it up and flung it into the fire. We don't need to be that severe with ourselves, but if you find that your mind has wandered completely away from the Prayer, just go back to the first word of that stanza and begin again. Adding to your repertoire of inspirational passages from the scriptures or great mystics will help to keep the words of the passage from growing stale.

After long and strenuous endeavor, the day will come when the windows of your senses close down completely and you are able to meditate with one-pointed absorption on the Prayer. Saint Teresa of Avila described this stage vividly:

> You will at once feel your senses gather themselves together; they seem like bees which return to the hive and then shut themselves up to work at the making of honey; and this will take place without effort or care on your part. God thus rewards the violence which your soul has been doing to itself, and gives to it such a domination over the senses that a sign is enough, when it desires to recollect itself, for them to obey and so gather themselves together. At the first call of the will they come back more and more quickly. At last, after many and many exercises of this kind, God disposes them to a state of absolute repose and of perfect contemplation.

In this book I give a practical commentary on passages for meditation from four great Christian exponents of what I call "love in action." My hope is to make these passages more meaningful for those who want to meditate on them and then translate their ideals into action. But although I often comment line for line, let me repeat that what I am recommending you do in meditation is very different. When you go through these words in meditation, your mind will want to follow all kinds of associations. This is not getting absorbed in the Prayer; it is wandering away from it. As you meditate on these precious words, give them all your attention. Gradually they will become part of you, reflected in everything you say and do.

The central principle of meditation is that we become what we meditate on. Over time, the transformation taking place in our character and consciousness is bound to show itself in our daily relations. Part of this transformation is accomplished in meditation, but the rest is done during the day. Meditation generates power that needs to be put to constructive use, particularly in healing our relationships. Francis once said that we pray to partake of the peace of the Lord, but that the hours of the day are meant for spreading this peace in the places where people dwell. When things go wrong at home, for instance, we need to try to remain patient and sympathetic. When someone at work is curt to us, we need to harness the strength found in meditation to move closer and show that person some special kindness.

power. By and large, it is good not to make up your own version of the Holy Name but to use a formula that has been sanctioned by centuries of devout tradition. Most words and phrases denote something to us only at relatively superficial levels of awareness; below that, in the unconscious, they mean nothing. If you repeat the Holy Name sincerely and systematically, however, you can verify for yourself that it goes deeper with every repetition. It can be with you even in the uttermost depths of your consciousness, as you will discover for yourself when you find it reverberating in a dream – or, deeper still, during dreamless sleep. When you awake, the thrill of this great experience will remain with you, reminding and inspiring and enabling you to be a little calmer and kinder throughout that day.

In the case of Saint Francis, we find this practice arising spontaneously from the depths of his ardent love. The *Fioretti* or *Little Flowers of Saint Francis,* the earliest collection we have of stories about Francis and the early Order, relates that the nobleman Bernard of Quintavalle, before he enlisted himself as a disciple, wanted to find out for himself whether young Francis of Assisi was a sincere lover of God; so he invited him to his wealthy home.

"Saint Francis accepted the invitation," the chronicle continues,

> and took supper with him, and stayed the night also; and then Bernard resolved to make trial of his

sanctity. He got a bed prepared for him in his own room, in which a lamp was always burning all night. Saint Francis, in order to conceal his sanctity, entered the room and immediately threw himself on the bed and feigned to sleep. Bernard also resolved to lie down, and began to snore loudly, as if in a very deep slumber.

Thereupon Saint Francis, believing that Bernard was really asleep, immediately rose from the bed and betook himself to prayer, and raising his eyes and his hands to heaven with the greatest devotion he said, "My God and my all!" So saying, and shedding many tears, he remained until morning, constantly repeating "My God and my all!" and nothing more.

Meditation and the repetition of the Holy Name go hand in hand: meditation is for the quiet hours of morning and evening; the Holy Name can be used at any other time of day or night. Together these two help us to change negative habits at a depth our ordinary will cannot reach. Francis once said that our knowledge is as deep as our action. Many people are victims of habits, such as smoking or drinking, which they know to be harmful, but still they are unable to give them up. If this knowledge is driven deeper into their consciousness through meditation and the Holy Name, it can free them from the tyranny of undesirable habits to follow wiser patterns of behavior. One of Francis's contemporaries, an historian who had been a student at Bologna and heard Francis speak on the Feast of the Assumption, described him in this way:

His habit was dirty, his appearance insignificant, his face not handsome. But God gave his words such power that many noble families, between whom there had been much old-time enmity and spilled blood, allowed themselves to be induced to make peace. And all felt great devotion and reverence for him. . . . He was not silent about wrongs that he saw, but gave everything its right name. And it seemed to each who listened that the poor little man from Assisi talked to him alone, as if all the words he heard were directed to him, and one after another, like well-aimed arrows sent by a master hand, thrust their points into his heart.

This is precisely what we experience in meditation as the holy words of Saint Francis's Prayer penetrate our hearts.

Let me now try to bring out some of the practical profundity of these words, drawing on my own experience.

[2]

Without spending a single moment beating about the bush, Francis comes straight to the point of the spiritual life: *Lord, make me an instrument of thy peace.* Our first priority is to reform ourselves; without that, how can we expect to help other people reform themselves? It is the living example of a man or woman giving every moment to making love a reality that moves our hearts to follow. We do not have to call ourselves religious to serve as examples of love and unity. We do not need a bumper sticker that says, "You are following an instrument of the Lord." Our everyday actions speak for themselves.

Just as the example of Jesus inspired Francis a millennium later, Francis inspired thousands of people even during his own lifetime. Near the end of his life, while he was making a mountain journey, Francis's health failed. His companions went into a farmyard to borrow a donkey for him to ride. On hearing for whom it was intended, the peasant came out and asked, "Are you the Brother Francis there is so much said about?" Receiving a nod from one of Francis's companions, he added, "Then take care that you are as good in reality as they say, for there are many who have confidence in you." Deeply stirred, Francis kissed the peasant in gratitude for this reminder of just how much such an example could mean even to people he had never met.

How can we go about making ourselves such an example? To begin with, as long as we are full of ourselves, our own small desires and self-centered thoughts, we leave no room whatever for the Lord to work in our lives. Jesus says simply, "Thy will be done." The implication is clear: to live in harmony with the divine will, our petty, selfish, personal will – self-will – has to go. When we ask to be made instruments of peace, what we are really asking for is the boundless determination to empty ourselves of every ugly state of mind that disrupts relationships – anger, resentment, jealousy, greed, self-will in any form.

Transforming these negative states of mind into their positive counterparts is not at all an easy task. Selfish desires and resentments masquerade as part of us, part of our personality. In reality they are only a mask, which can be removed to reveal our real personality. Mystics call this mask self-will. I often call it the ego. Either name means the self-centered drive to get what I want, have my own way, whatever the cost to others. This is the source of all selfish and destructive behavior.

In English fiction there is a fascinating character known as the Scarlet Pimpernel. He shows up here, then there, then here again, breaking the law for what he considers worthy causes, but the authorities can never lay eyes on him. That is how the ego behaves. It simply is not possible to challenge him to a duel. He will not reply to your invitation; he will never pick up your gauntlet; if you shout at him, your echo will shout back at you. But there are a million little ways in which you can slowly track the ego to its lair.

If someone were to pull over to the side of the road in San Francisco and ask me how to get to Los Angeles, I wouldn't say, "Go north." Everyone knows you have to go the other direction. Similarly, spiritual figures like Saint Francis tell us, "Don't follow your selfish desires and angry impulses; that is the way to emotional bankruptcy." But we reply, "Oh, no! I know what I'm doing. It's obvious which way is better." Francis would insist, "Please believe me. If you go that way, you will become more insecure. People will slowly lose their respect for you, and you will lose respect for yourself. Eventually you will not feel at home anywhere on earth. Instead, let me show you a secret trail that will take you slowly round so you can surprise the ego in his sleep. He'll never know what hit him."

Like most people I have met in this country, I too was conditioned at an early age by talk about not "repressing" the ego. I believed that if you defy a strong selfish impulse, sooner or later your frustrations will explode. The lives of men and women like Saint Francis, however, show us just the opposite: reducing the ego for the sake of fulfilling a higher goal, a loftier desire than self-interest, is not repression but transformation. The signs are sure. Repression bottles up our energy, so that it can make itself felt only in destructive ways. When this energy is transformed, however, it is released every day in creative ways that we can see: patience, resilience under stress, skill in building bridges between others and ourselves.

When a selfish urge is crying out for satisfaction, then, that is an ideal opportunity to summon up your will and go against that urge. Because so much of our vital energy is caught up in pampering these selfish impulses, they offer us a long, long trail right into the depths of consciousness. When we defy the impulse and use its energy for some selfless purpose, we are following a trail that will eventually allow us to get around the ego.

These are the dynamics of spiritual transformation. The route is always there and it is always open; that is its promise. We must be prepared for many, many years of arduous hiking over rough terrain. Very likely we are going to have lapses; some very attractive detours may distract us temporarily. All that we are asking the Lord for is the determination to do our best to stay on the right trail and go forward.

As a practical first step toward becoming an instrument of peace, we can try our best not to harbor grudges. One suggestion is that when you have a falling-out with someone, instead of deciding on the spot that you are not going to come within ten feet of that person, try going out for a really fast walk, repeating the Holy Name in your mind until the immediate wave of anger rolls over you. (If a fast walk is not feasible, sit down quietly to repeat the Name.) Then you can make a simple effort to recall some of the good things that person has done for you. He may have let it go by when you said something particularly unkind to him one time; or perhaps when you got sick she took care of you. Anger makes us utterly forget all these incidents, so that for a while we see only the dark side. When we remind ourselves that even though at present we may be nursing a very real injury, the past has brought us kindness and aid from this person, our anger will find it difficult to burn for very long.

On another front, I have come to feel that one of the cornerstones of peaceful relations everywhere is the capacity to avoid becoming wedded to one's own opinions. Francis repeatedly warned his brothers about trying to "embrace poverty while keeping the purse of your own opinion." When we do not have this capacity, arrogance often makes its ugly appearance. At the mere hint of disagreement we get agitated, and our views are liable to come out clothed in harsh tones and intemperate language. The message to the other party is clear: we have scant respect for him or her as a person. Nothing wounds more deeply or muddies the original issue more thoroughly. It is then that war breaks out. We need not think of war only in terms of the War of the Roses or the landing on the beaches of Normandy. Skirmishes are fought in the dining room all the time; guerrilla warfare is often waged in the kitchen.

Where there is hatred, let me sow love.

To the south of my ancestral home in Kerala, South India, beautiful rice fields stretch almost to the horizon. When I was a little boy, every morning during the planting season I would be awakened just after dawn by the sounds of the villagers plowing the land with their bullocks, talking and singing as they worked. First the tiny seedlings must be planted.

Somebody goes along with a big basket, planting them one by one in a row, so carefully that when you look at rice growing, it looks like a gigantic green carpet. Later each seedling must be transplanted. All in all, it is difficult to believe that these minute seedlings are going to bear such a rich harvest.

You and I can go in for a similar kind of hand labor. When you plant just one kind word with somebody who has been unkind to you, though it is only a tiny seedling, it is going to bear a rich harvest. A lot of people get the benefit — secondhand, thirdhand, fourthhand — from our little kindnesses. Every time you focus on what brings people together instead of what drives them apart, you are planting a long row of these seedlings. Every day — in the office, at school, in the kitchen, at the store — everyone has opportunities for this kind of hand labor. We may think our opportunities are hardly worth the trouble, but little things like kindness catch on and spread.

In Kerala we have a giant, fierce-looking plant called elephant nettle. It seems to flourish in every nook and cranny, and you have only to walk by for it to stretch out to touch you. One little touch and you feel as if you have been stung. By the time you get home, you have a blister that won't let you think about anything else until it goes away.

My grandmother, my spiritual teacher, was expert at driving home great truths with homely illustrations. She used to say, "A self-willed person is like an elephant nettle." That is why the moment we see somebody who is given to saying unkind things, we make a detour. We pretend we have just remembered something that takes us in another direction, but the fact is that we just don't want to be stung. "I promise not to go near the elephant nettles," I always assured my granny. But when it came to a classmate I did not like, she would say, "Here, you have to learn to grow. Go near him. Let yourself slowly get comfortable around him; then give him your sympathy and help take the sting out of his nettleness."

I am not one of those philosophical people who say, "No matter what you do to me, it is all right." Certainly not! When someone is being unkind, whether to me or to somebody else, I feel a loving obligation to remonstrate with him, kindly but firmly. When a person senses that we have his best interests at heart, when he knows we will not move away from him whatever distress he is causing, we can remonstrate and at the same time support him in his efforts to overcome his problem.

Where there is injury, pardon.

When children cry, my mother used to remind me, they are really trying to speak to us. They have some problem and do not know how to explain what is bothering them, so they use the only language they have: lifting the roof off. Grown-ups usually go in for a more subtle style. When they get really annoyed, they let loose with some choice epithets, stalk out of the house (often tripping over the threshold), and growl something rude to the first person they see. We understand this more easily than an infant's tantrum, but it is just as childish. When a baby raises the roof, most people do not respond by taking it personally and getting hostile; they try to find out what the problem is and solve it. Saint Francis is reminding us that there is no more reason to take grown-ups' annoyance personally than we do children's.

No one would claim for a second that this kind of response comes easily. Dealing with acrimonious situations and self-willed people with a calm patience requires toughness, the inner toughness that real love demands. In matters like these, one of Francis's earliest disciples, Brother Juniper, won a reputation for his naive ingenuity. Once, when a superior reprimanded him with great severity, Brother Juniper was so disturbed by the grief he had caused that in the middle of the night he jumped out of bed, prepared some porridge with a big lump of butter on top, and took it to his superior's room. "Father," he said, standing at the door with the bowl of porridge in one hand and a lighted candle in the other, "today when you reprimanded me I noticed that you were hoarse from excitement. Now I have prepared this porridge for you and beg you to eat it; it is good for the throat and chest."

The superior impatiently told Brother Juniper to go away and let him sleep.

"Well," said Brother Juniper simply, "the porridge is cooked and has to be eaten, so please be so kind as to hold the light while I do the eating." His superior must have laughed in spite of himself, and we are told that he was sporting enough to sit down with Brother Juniper so they could eat the porridge together.

Most of us will never be so ingenuous as Brother Juniper, but we can still learn to head off resentment in every way possible. The more resentment is allowed to grow, the more damage it is going to do. Resentment is like swallowing a seed from the elephant nettle: soon our whole insides will ache from top to bottom from its stinging, and we won't have the vaguest idea how to get rid of it. Just think about the comparison a little. Not only will that resentment wreak havoc with our emotional well-being, it will gradually break down the functioning of our physical system as well.

Resentment will defend itself with a foolish argument: "Well, it's my own business." Not at all. In the first place, unless the person against whom you nurse the grudge is extremely secure, you are making that person into an agitated missile who is going to injure a lot of others. This is no exaggeration. Resentment is contagious, much more so than a virus. In a home where it is allowed to fester, everybody gets infected: the children, the children's playmates, even the dog. But kindness is even more contagious. Whenever people see somebody facing harsh treatment with quiet security, with a kind of infectious good humor, they get infected too. "How I wish I could do that!" they marvel. We can use kindness to inoculate those around us against the dread disease of resentment.

Where there is doubt, faith; where there is despair, hope.

I keep up with a variety of magazines and newspapers, and I find a lot of people throwing up their hands. Many tell us civilization is doomed, perhaps even the planet itself. I am not one of those who claim all is well no matter what is happening. On many fronts, the horizon *is* dark. But who is responsible for all these crises? Not the three Greek sisters of fate, not the Power which created us. It is we ourselves who are totally responsible; therefore it is we who can set these wrong situations right.

The shining examples of spiritual figures like Saint Francis stand as monuments of hope. They had to face adversities of every description, opposition from every imaginable kind of entrenched self-interest. Often they were able to make use of such problems to spur themselves on. When we take a good look at the state of the world, we are sometimes inclined to say, "There is nothing to be done." If we would only turn to the example of Saint Francis we would have to admit, "It's not impossible, really. Look what he was able to accomplish. Why can't we manage some of the same?"

When I was in India, I came across a number of American expressions that baffled me. One was "pulling yourself up by your own bootstraps." I resolved that when I came to this country, I would look for some person performing this acrobatic feat! This is the marvel of meditation – a marvel I have never been able to get over. Nobody pulls you up; you pull yourself up. It should appeal enormously to the justly lauded spirit of American ingenuity. Francis himself said, "More than all grace and all the gifts of the Holy Spirit . . . is the conquering of yourself." You go to work on your own mind and change whatever needs changing, making yourself into the kind of person most suited to meeting the challenges of the day. There is cause for enormous hope here.

None of us need be ashamed or embarrassed if ghosts out of our past come and whisper, "Remember what you did in high school? All the escapades you took part in? How unkind you were, how you wasted so many opportunities?" To me, this sort of guilt is a trick the ego plays to make us doubt ourselves. It is most unfair. Here we are looking back at our behavior of ten or twenty or thirty years ago and judging it by our standards of today. Who has not made mistakes at some tumultuous period in life? If you ask me personally, "Did you?" I will say, "Plenty." And if you ask, "Well, don't you too feel guilty about what you did?" I will say, "I'm not proud of it, but that is how I saw life then."

If you want to judge yourself, the only fair way is to judge yourself with today's eyes as you are today. Look at yourself straight on and ask, "Have I been selfish today in any way?" If you have a competitive streak, this is where you can make good use of it. Just say, "Today in such and such ways I have been somewhat selfish, but tomorrow I'll do better."

Where there is darkness, light.

On a dark night when you are stumbling along the road trying to pick your way home, what would you say if somebody came up and offered to help with a flashlight that has no battery? People who are quick to anger or who nurse grudges have no battery in their flashlight; we would do well to tell them, "Please don't bring your flashdark here." Isn't there a battery called Eveready? Well, resentful people have a battery that can be called Neveready. By refusing to let their compassion shine, they darken the path of everyone around them. On the other hand, people who are patient and who can love you more than they love themselves have a flashlight that shines in all directions at the same time.

There are many different sizes of flashlights. I have one by my bedside which is the size of a fountain pen. I can hardly see anything with it, but it is better than the dark; at least it shows you where the walls are so that you avoid walking into them and banging your head. That is the first stage of our transformation: we appear as little fountain pens of light. A group at a party is saying, "I can't see any good in Ebenezer at all," and we chime in, "Oh, he has helped me out a few times."

As we are able to work more comfortably and

harmoniously with people, we will find that instead of a penlight we hold a normal, hand-sized flashlight. People begin to look to us for advice and solace. They like to be around us because we somehow make them feel more secure. Finally, when we see the spark of divinity burning in the people around us, we are like a big beacon. People are drawn to us, because they find that by our light their paths become clear and well marked.

Where there is sadness, joy.

This line touches me deeply. Saint Francis is quietly bringing home to us a tremendous responsibility. Our influence, whether for sadness or for joy, reaches everywhere. We cannot ever say, "I live alone in an attic off Fourth Street. This line does not apply to me." Don't you ride on a bus where thirty people see how solemn and sad you look? Everywhere we go we affect people.

Once a student of mine in India thought he had found an answer to this. I met him on campus and said to him casually, "I've been noticing how downcast you look these days. It grieves me. Is there anything I can do?"

"There is no need for you to be concerned about the way I look," he replied politely enough. "It's my face." "Yes," I agreed, "it is your face. But it is we who have to look at it."

Francis himself was far from being a solemn-faced ascetic. Often he went about singing softly, and on the road he liked to regale his companions with songs of God's glories which he composed himself – in French, the language of the troubadours. "We Friars Minor," he exclaimed once, "what are we except God's singers and players, who seek to draw hearts upwards and to fill them with spiritual joy?" Their joy was so great that "when they returned from their work at evening time or when in the course of the day met on the road, love and joy shone out of their eyes, and they greeted each other with chaste embraces, holy kisses, cheerful words, modest smiles. . . ."

[3]

Francis's second stanza begins beautifully: *O divine Master. . . .* We can all think of ourselves as the Lord's footmen and handmaids; he is the Master, the one and only boss. It is a superstition to believe that we are unemployed at any time. We are all born with our appointment orders: "You, Morton E. Hazelby, are hereby instructed to contribute to life on earth and continue contributing until the last breath of the life I have given you is spent." Those of us who take the terms of this order to heart become secure and respected wherever we go.

The ideal of living as the Lord's servant was embodied with consummate grace by Francis's dear disciple Clare. Though she held the office of abbess and all the Sisters at tiny San Damiano convent looked up to her as their spiritual leader, it was Clare who most often served them at table, pouring water over their hands and waiting upon them. She took personal care of any Brothers and Sisters who happened to be sick, and did not hesitate to take on any chore, however lowly, that needed doing. When Sisters came home from working outside the convent, Clare washed their feet with her holy hands. And at night she often got up to put the covers back on a Sister who had uncovered herself in her sleep, for fear she might become chilled.

> *Grant that I may not so much seek to be consoled as to console.*

Beggars, lepers, all who suffered were sacred in Saint Francis's eyes. Whatever he had he would willingly give to someone more in need. Often he gave away his hood, a part of his habit, or even his trousers to beggars, so that his companions had their work cut out for them just keeping clothes on their beloved Francis's back. But there was a deeper object in his giving too. One day in Perugia he met a man he had formerly known who was now reduced to utter poverty. The man complained with great bitterness at having been treated so unjustly by his master. "I will willingly give you my hood," begged Francis, "if you will forgive your master his injustice." The man's heart was moved. He forgot his hatred, it is said, and was filled with the sweetness of forgiveness.

As a boy, when I was feeling sorry for myself because of difficulties in school or with someone in the village, my grandmother used to tell me gently, "This is not sorrow; this is self-pity. Self-pity weakens, but sorrow for others strengthens and ennobles human nature." This is a distinction worth remembering, particularly in times of distress. Whenever we feel life has been hard on us, instead of going off to our bed-room and locking the door, that is the ideal time for turning our grief outward and putting it to work as compassion for the sorrows of others. After all, every-one faces misfortunes in life – now and again, severe ones. If, in the midst of our own troubles, we can go to a grieving neighbor or to someone sick and offer help, we will find that while we are lifting their spirits, we are lifting our own as well. This is a perfect recipe both for nipping depression in the bud and for spreading consolation.

To be understood as to understand.

When I first took to meditation, my attitude toward my students underwent a substantial change. You know, when you have been talking in class for five days running about Wordsworth's view of nature and on Friday you ask one or two simple questions and can get no satisfactory answer, it is natural to feel a bit exasperated. "Why can't they follow?" I used to ask myself. "Or, if they can't follow, why can't they at least read through the text at home so they can answer simple questions?"

Gradually, however, I began to develop a more compassionate attitude. It struck me forcefully that words like Saint Francis's were meant not only to be repeated in meditation but to be applied, even in mundane situations on a university campus. I began to understand, for example, that it was unreasonable to expect a good performance from a student who had an irresistible tendency to daydream and procrastinate. With that insight, my exasperation evaporated. I saw such problems now from my students' perspective, and instead of wishing they were different, my attention went to getting to know those students and helping them learn better habits. Teaching became a matter of not merely conveying knowledge, but of showing how to live.

Understanding is the first thing to jump out the window when two emotionally involved people get into a quarrel. "He just doesn't understand me!" is a grumble that frequently reaches my ears. Saint Francis, I suspect, would reply, "What does it matter? The real question is, do you understand him? Have you tried to understand his point of view?" The honest answer would usually be no. Strong emotions plug up our ears like those foam earplugs which expand into the opening of your ear to prevent even a single wave of sound from getting through.

I have yet to hear of anyone who did not understand his or her own side of a quarrel in minute detail. "See, my hay fever is acting up now because my prescription ran out, and I had this terrific headache from our youngest son yelling at me. So when my husband came into the kitchen and slammed the door for no reason, I just let him have it." Our private prosecuting attorney in the mind has built up an open-and-shut case. That is the problem: we shut the case too soon. As any experienced judge knows, every case has two sides. Fairness demands that we give equal time to the defense, who is inside us too. The other side deserves the same hearing and the same benefit of the doubt that we give ourselves as a matter of course. This is detachment. If we can practice it, quarrels can be settled amicably before they ever come before a jury.

To be loved as to love.

Now we get down to the nitty-gritty of romance. Millions of people today voice the heartfelt complaint that they feel lonely and unloved. It is a serious condition. Here Saint Francis is saying, "I know the cause of the malady and I know the secret of its complete cure." No matter what the relationship may be, when you look on another person as someone who can give you love, you are really *faking* love. That is the simplest word for it. If you are interested in making love, in making it grow without end, try looking on that person as someone you can give your love to – someone to whom you can go on giving always.

Learning to love is like swimming against the current of a powerful river; most of our conditioning is in the other direction. When the river by my village used to flood with the advent of the monsoon rains, we boys liked to try to swim across without being swept downstream by the current. To tell you the truth, I never succeeded. The only time I came close was the time someone told me there was a crocodile after me. But a few of my cousins were such powerful swimmers that they could fight the current and reach the other side exactly opposite from where they had set out. It is simply a question of developing your muscles: the more you use them, the stronger they get. Similarly, when you put the other person's welfare foremost every day, no matter how strong the opposing tide inside, you discover after a while that you can love a little more today than you did yesterday. Tomorrow you will be able to love a little more.

There is no end to love. It does not confine itself to just one person or one family. Most of us seem to feel that if Romeo, say, begins to care deeply for Juliet's nurse, his love for Juliet will somehow be diminished; Juliet should feel jealous. If he learns to extend his love to her brothers, the nurse should feel neglected too. There is no conflict. Romeo still loves Juliet and still cares for her nurse; it is just that he is coming to love everybody. He can be completely loyal to his sweetheart, Juliet, and completely loyal in all his other relationships as well. The beauty of this kind of love is that it never divides; it will bring Juliet, her nurse, and her brothers closer together than they ever were before.

For it is in giving that we receive.

This is one of the most incredible paradoxes in life. We think, naturally enough, that if we go after what we want, we will probably get it; then we will be happy and secure. The mass media intone this line of thinking like a litany: grab, grab, grab! Yet sooner or later the whole smorgasbord of things to get causes every sensitive person to ask, "If I go on grabbing and grabbing, at what point is it that I become secure and feel no more need to grab?" This question can lead to some far-reaching answers. Our needs are much too big to be satisfied with things, no matter how many we can manage to acquire. Often, it seems, the more we try to get, the more acutely we feel those needs.

We are used today to thinking in terms of presents – Father's Day presents, Mother's Day presents, birth-day presents, Christmas presents. The great excite-ment at Christmas is looking in our stocking and opening gifts. Francis might ask, "Don't you want to find your stocking filled with good things every morning?" We *can,* every morning after meditation. But we cannot expect to find our stocking filled if we leave it hanging there full of stuff. There will be no room for the Lord to put anything in unless we empty ourselves every day by giving all we can in the way of kindness and loving help. Then every morning we will find ourselves full again – of love, of understand-ing, of forgiveness, of energy with which to carry these gifts to others. Saint Francis has been telling us in every line of this Prayer that this is the Lord's way of giving: the more we share what we have, the more he wants to give us from within.

Every day we can receive these gifts and every day we can share them, whether people are friendly to us or not. The more we share, the more we will win the love and respect of others – and the more we win their love and respect, the less our turmoil and troubles. Personal burdens will lie lightly on us. Our deepest need is for the joy that comes with loving and being loved, with knowing we are of genuine use to others. For everybody who has problems or who wants to go forward steadily on the spiritual path, my recipe would be to do more for others and think less about yourself. Hang up an empty stocking and every day you will find your life filling more and more with joy.

It is in pardoning that we are pardoned.

Late in his life Francis found himself com-pelled to give over his place as head of the order to Brother Elias, who thereafter became very keen on improving the conduct of his Brothers. When Elias came to him with complaints and plans to penalize some of them, Francis gave him strong advice: "See to it that no Brother in the whole world, however he may have sinned, is permitted to go from you without forgiveness if he asks for it. And if he does not ask for forgiveness, then ask him if he does not want it. And even if he comes before your eyes a thousand times with sin, love him more than you do me, that you may draw him to the Lord; . . . for the healthy need no physician, but only those who suffer illness."

The forgiveness Francis is prescribing here is not a matter merely of saying "I forgive you; let bygones be bygones." No amount of talking can prevent the seed of resentment from taking hold in our heart. True forgiveness requires that we not only not take personally any harsh thing said or done to us, but that we make an all-out effort to understand the other person's situation. Then, even if we get angry for a few minutes and think, "That Mortimer!" we know it will soon turn to "Well, he comes from a discordant home, and nobody showed him how to object nicely." When this happens, we know that resentment doesn't stand a chance. But Francis is zealous in his recommendation that we follow up this forgiving with genuine acts of kindness, which can actually cure the impulse of the other person to say or do something harsh again.

It is in dying to self that we are born to eternal life.

We all have deep within us an overwhelming desire to lose ourselves in love. In practical terms, this is what loving the Lord means. Saint Francis is reminding us again that the way to live in the presence of the Lord is to find that love which flows all the time, regardless of people's ups and downs, which brings together not only our own dear ones but all others as well. Finding this love requires a lot of labor and anguish, but it is this labor, which we accomplish by meditating and incorporating the other spiritual disciplines into our daily life, that opens the floodgates of love.

Loving the Lord has the miraculous power to change us. We all know how, when a young man feels drawn to a young lady, his personal appearance improves overnight, his language becomes more refined, his taste in reading and entertainment takes on a softer, more romantic bent. In the same way, as we begin to understand better what pleases the Lord, our personality begins to change. We make more of an effort to be patient with people, and even if anger does come up, it has less sting. We start to sympathize with the difficulties others are facing. This is an inescapable transformation.

If you ask lovers of God how they can find joy in effacing themselves, they will tell you, "Otherwise, I don't stand a chance; my Lord won't even look at me. He will say, 'Who wants this angry grouch around?' This gives us all the determination we need to empty ourselves. When we succeed, even a little, we feel ourselves moving that much closer to him." They do not deny that this can be distressing, but they assure us that the joy we find in this growing love will give us motivation to face distress with equanimity.

In time, we begin to enrich our life with concern for everybody, with giving our time and our energy to helping others. By directing our attention to others' welfare, we make our own life fuller and more beautiful. This is the source of the incredibly selfless, undemanding love we see in someone like Saint Francis, which seems to us so uncanny. It is what Saint Bernard was hinting at when he explained, "I love because I love; I love in order that I may love." *When I do not love,* he is trying to tell us, *I am parted from my Lord; and that I cannot bear.*

Introduction by Carol Lee Flinders

Threading her way carefully along the run-down sidewalks of San Francisco's Mission District, between the stumbling derelicts and the weary bag ladies, the dull-eyed, bewildered adolescents and the children – silent, thin, and much too wary – there passes a young woman dressed so distinctively that even here, in this motleyest of neighborhoods, one notices her. She is a nun. Her head is veiled, a crucifix hangs at her left shoulder, and she wears the blue-bordered white sari of the Missionaries of Charity, known better, though not officially, as the Sisters of Mother Teresa of Calcutta.

In all the United States, there is no city more expensive to live in than San Francisco. To be poor in San Francisco is therefore particularly arduous. That is one reason why the Missionaries of Charity have come here, to the city named (the irony was never intended, and by most it's still not sensed) after Saint Francis. It was among some of the most desperately impoverished people on earth that Mother Teresa began her work of love, and now that members of her order have been invited into cities around the world, they still work, for the most part, among the poorest and hungriest.

The physical privations of San Francisco's less-than-lucky account only in part, though, for the presence of the Missionaries of Charity. One could cite places that have not been so blessed where the apparent need is greater. But the poverty of the West, Mother Teresa believes, falls with a special weight, and cuts with its own keen edge:

> When I pick up a person from the street, hungry, I give him a plate of rice, a piece of bread, and I have removed that hunger. But a person that is shut out, that feels unwanted, unloved, terrified, the person that has been thrown out from society — that poverty is so hurtable and so much, and I find that very difficult. Our Sisters are working amongst that kind of people in the West.

Just as Saint Francis did in creating the Third Order, Mother Teresa has opened the way for people of all situations in life to participate in her work. Some are formally organized as Co-Workers, who meet regularly to pray together and who assist in the work materially by collecting clothing, making bandages, and fitting out the dispensaries. But in the widest sense, we all have a role to play.

To the work carried out by the Missionaries of Charity among the most destitute people in India and elsewhere, not everyone is called. But where that other kind of poverty is concerned, "The poverty of the spirit, of loneliness and being unwanted," whose consequences are ultimately just as serious, there, she insists, we all have a vocation. "This is the hunger you and I must find," Mother Teresa reminds us, "and it may be in our own home."

Her counsel is simple and direct. Begin where you are, she tells us — extend your love to the people right around you. Fill your homes with love and let that love radiate outward. "We must make our homes centers of compassion," she says, "and forgive endlessly." And she makes what some might think a very tall claim:

> I think the world today is upside-down, and is suffering so much, because there is so very little love in the homes and in family life. We have no time for our children, we have no time for each other; there is no time to enjoy each other. If we could only bring back into our lives the life that Jesus, Mary and Joseph lived in Nazareth, if we could make our homes another Nazareth, I think that peace and joy would reign in the world.

When the Nobel Prize for Peace was given to Mother Teresa in 1979, the award announcement commended her "for work undertaken in the struggle to overcome poverty and distress in the world, which also constitute a threat to peace." To give public recognition to the role that hunger and homelessness have in causing war was a very good thing for the Committee to have done. It is interesting, though, that Mother Teresa herself did not speak in quite those terms — said nothing about how if people have enough to eat, and clothing to wear, they're not as likely to enter into war.

Instead, in a characteristically broken but impassioned rush of eloquence, she appealed to every one of us: "And I think that we in our family — we don't need bombs and guns to destroy. To bring peace, just get together, love one another, bring that peace, that joy, that strength of presence of each other in the home. And we will be able to overcome all the evil that is in the world."

Which is to say, Mother Teresa believes in miracles, or at least in what might seem miraculous today. She believes, for she has experienced it and watched it in others, that within each of us is an enormous, indomitable power for good. Her version of peace goes far beyond the absence of war — and that is why she is such a powerful force for peace.

Reflecting on the subtle change that took place in Calcutta as awareness of Mother Teresa's work spread, one observer has remarked that it was as though for the first time, in that city of bottomless need, there was a safety net. In Mother Teresa's own words, "Ordinary people are beginning to get concerned. Before, they used to pass by a person dying on the streets, but now, when they see something like that, they immediately do something. If they can't get an ambulance, they bring the person to us by rickshaw, or taxi, or take them to Kalighat, or they phone us. The big thing is that they do something; it's wonderful, eh?"

The image of a safety net applies to the Missionaries of Charity in an even deeper sense, though, well beyond the good they do directly and consciously. That is because, in the quietest, most unassuming way possible, without saying a word, they challenge the view of human nature on which contemporary civilization rests — and with it, all the cynicism and despair that flow from that view. They "bear witness" to a very different picture.

Not everyone grasps what these sisters mean when they say "We do it for Jesus," or when they paraphrase his words: "In the poor it is the hungry Christ that we are feeding, it is the naked Christ that we are clothing, it is to the homeless Christ that we are giving shelter." Words are only words, after all. Yet the meaning comes through. Describing a visit to one of Mother Teresa's Homes in Calcutta, one writer recalls "a young American who was plainly radiating God's love. . . . He was administering to the particularly wretched cases with a tenderness other men his age use to express their first breathless outpourings of love. He was from New York, a Jew; he had traveled all over but, man, he had never seen anything like this. So beautiful, so beautiful."

At every opportunity, Mother Teresa reiterates the endlessly astonishing fact about the work — the fact this young man from New York had unwittingly stumbled upon and that Saint Francis put so simply: "It is in giving that we receive." Going forth in love, reaching out with love, they have found, in men and women who have every reason to behave otherwise, courage, gratitude, and enormous sweetness. And out of this experience comes a rock-solid faith — infectious, highly communicable, shining out from the eyes of everyone who possesses it — in the essential goodness of us all.

Mother Teresa describes a man brought to them, near death, who said, "I have lived like an animal in the street, but I am going to die like an angel, loved and cared for."

"And it was so wonderful," she adds, "to see the greatness of that man who could speak like that, who could die like that without blaming anybody, without cursing anybody ... this is the greatness of our people. And that is why we believe what Jesus has said: 'I was hungry — I was naked — I was homeless ...'"

Strip away the highly-colored facade of life today, slow down its heated pace so you can get a good look, and it's easy enough to see the assumptions that underlie it — assumptions that add up to a definite view of human nature: that we are finite, limited, and essentially powerless creatures, defined by our needs and desires, compelled in a world of scarcity to fight for them, and successful to the extent we gratify them.

It's a dismal verdict, reinforced by books, films, advertisements, and it has eroded every tender and sturdy bond that ever linked us one to another. Can a phrase like "the family of man" have any resonance at all, any power to move us, if the word "family" has none? Mother Teresa doubts it.

So much of what goes on under the name of peace work is in fact simply anti-war work. But what Mother Teresa suggests, implicitly as well as in words, is that the greatest, most effective and powerful way to oppose war is to wage peace — to wage love — to pour out your energy and concern from a source that is, in fact, endless.

Easwaran's essay on Mother Teresa addresses that basic challenge she sets before us: love. He is a seasoned teacher, and he knows very well that in the heart of his hearer one question is reverberating: "But how? How can I take this very limited and ineffectual self and make it into a powerful force for good?"

"Thou shalt love the Lord thy God with thy whole heart, with thy whole soul, and with thy whole mind." This is the commandment of the great God, and he cannot command the impossible.

Love is a fruit in season at all times, and within reach of every hand. Anyone may gather it and no limit is set. Everyone can reach this love through meditation, spirit of prayer, and sacrifice, by an intense inner life.

Hunger for Love

There is hunger for ordinary bread, and there is hunger for love, for kindness, for thoughtfulness; and this is the great poverty that makes people suffer so much.

Our modern civilization is so physically oriented that when we hear the word hunger, we immediately think in terms of vitamins and minerals and amino acids. It seldom occurs to us that just as the body develops problems when it does not get adequate food, the person who is deprived of love – or worse, who finds it difficult to love – becomes subject to problems every bit as serious. I am not referring merely to emotional problems, though these of course are included. More and more evidence indicates that lack of love not only leads to loneliness, despair, and resentment, but eventually may even lead to deterioration of the vital organs. Researchers have made a good case for connecting cardiovascular accidents like heart attack with selfishness, isolation, alienation, and bereavement, all of which can be traced to lack of love. And a brilliant San Francisco cardiologist, Meyer Friedman, traces many cardiovascular problems to a syndrome of thought and behavior called "Type A personality," exhibited by men or women who are "aggressively involved in a chronic, incessant struggle to achieve more and more in less and less time, and if required to do so, against the opposing efforts of other things or other persons."

In fact, I would say, if they are allowed to continue, such ways of thinking and acting place us at risk for more than just cardiovascular problems. When we are continually driven by a strong desire to get something for ourselves – success, pleasure, reputation, power – we live in stress all day long, day in and day out, seven days a week. We grow increasingly anxious about getting what we want, and get angry more and more often when we can't get our way – all of which only makes the demands of our desires more fierce. The body adjusts to this state of stress by keeping adaptive mechanisms like elevated blood pressure switched on almost all the time. And after a while, not surprisingly, part of the system breaks down. The medical community would be precise: "Cause of death: myocardial infarction." That is a cause, but not the first cause. We could say with equal accuracy, "He died of greed and from always putting himself first. He died from never having learned to love."

In other words, when spiritual figures like Mother Teresa talk about our need to love and to be loved, the need is not metaphorical. Mother Teresa is not talking about spirituality alone; she is talking about good nutrition. Resentment, hostility, alienation, and selfishness are deficiency diseases. You can have all the essential amino acids, vitamins, and minerals known and unknown but if you cannot love, you are not likely to remain in good health.

We can think of Mother Teresa as a perfect physician. She has her protocols, set forth in the Sermon on the Mount and Saint Paul's "epistle on love," and the signs and symptoms of deficiency are all too easy to recognize. She puts a thermometer to modern industrial civilization, checks its blood pressure, and gives her diagnosis without hesitation: "Acute spiritual malnutrition. The patient is trying to meet all his needs with selfishness; love is crowded out." But malnutrition is reversible. Just as negative emotions like anger, fear, and greed have great power to harm, Mother Teresa knows what to prescribe to heal: good will, patience, overriding love for all.

We scarcely know today what this word *love* means. Most often it is used for physical relationships which have very little to do with love. Such relationships are based on physical satisfaction, which means that when the satisfaction goes – as all physical satisfactions must – the relationship falls apart. Love is not based on sensations; it is a lasting state of mind. At its highest – love pure and perfected, love that is completely selfless – it never asks what it can get but only what it can give. Physical sensation leads only to spiritual starvation; pure love nourishes and heals.

Usually a good physician will not write a prescription without some accompanying instructions: plenty of rest, lots of fluids, and so on. Certain conditions have to be fulfilled for the prescription to be most effective. Similarly, if love is prescribed as the remedy for our condition, to perfect pure love we need five things. The first is time. Second is control over our attention. Third comes energy, vitality. Fourth, we need discrimination. And fifth, we must have awareness of the unity of life.

Let me elaborate on these one by one.

Time

An obsession with time has been so worked into our social system that we scarcely notice we have left no time to love. Everywhere the slogan is Hurry, Hurry, Hurry. Yet to be aware of the needs of others, to spend time with others, to speak and act with patience and consideration, we must have time – a lot more time than most of us have at present.

On the one hand, this is a matter of simplifying our lives, dropping less important activities in order to allow more time for what matters most. But it is also essential to slow down our pace of living, so that we can free ourselves from the time-driven thinking and behavior characteristic of modern life.

One of the most effective steps to take here is simple: get up early. If you wake up late, rush through breakfast, run for the bus, and reach your office ten minutes after everyone else has settled down, that is

punctuated by long pauses while they search for a particular word, even to upset a glass of milk, and still get off to school on time; all this is part of a loving breakfast. In these terms, I suspect that there are few people today who have a truly loving breakfast. All too often the term is reserved for a doughnut or some precooked flakes of cellulose heated up in a microwave oven, which is neither loving nor a breakfast.

"You can afford to say 'Go slow,' Uncle," my little niece Geetha used to complain with exasperation. "You don't have to go to school." I have to confess that I took my time at meals even when I *did* have to go to school; it is something I probably absorbed from my grandmother, who never felt pressured. So even if it is your first day at high school, even if you have a big day at the office and a hundred things to accomplish before noon, let your breakfast be unhurried. There is never any need for an unkind word, a numb tongue, or a cold shoulder. If you do not have much to say, you can always listen with attention. And please do not read the newspaper at the table. Millions of people, I think, use the morning paper not so much for the news as for a shield. They are shielding themselves from love.

Mother Teresa, I was interested to see, draws the same unexpected connection between time and love. "Everybody today seems to be in such a terrible rush," she observes, "anxious for greater developments and greater riches and so on, so that children have very little time for their parents. Parents have very little time for each other, and in the home begins the disruption of the peace of the world."

Attention

Slowing down is closely connected with one-pointed attention: doing one thing at a time, and doing it with complete attention. In the case of rushing, for example, the problem is not only one of speed. Our attention is riveted on ourselves — *our* needs, *our* deadlines, *our* desires — so there is no attention to give to those around us, who have needs and desires and perhaps even deadlines very much like our own. Especially for children, we need to slow down so that we can give them our attention, which they require as much as food and sleep.

Meditation is essentially a matter of learning to direct and maintain a steady flow of attention. Then, during the day, we continue to train the mind by keeping it one-pointed on the job at hand.

Interestingly enough, a many-pointed mind seems to be characteristic of the Type A personality. Dr. Friedman called it by an exotic name, "polyphasic thinking," but it is extremely common, and not just among high-powered executives. Many people, for example, find it difficult to stay interested in anything except themselves. While they are listening to you and saying, "Yes, how true," their attention wanders away, and they start planning the evening's menu or doing a few stock market calculations in their head. When they are driving, instead of concentrating on the road, they turn on the radio and start going over some old memory or rehearsing an argument with the boss. In such cases, there is no focus of attention. The mind is jumping about like a grasshopper, and there is no control over it.

Through practicing meditation and giving full concentration to one thing at a time, we can learn to direct attention where we choose. This is an almost miraculous skill, with applications to the practice of love that are as simple as they are essential. When we can give complete attention to the person we are with, even if she is contradicting our opinions on tax reform or explaining the peculiarities of Roman law, boredom disappears from our relationships. People are not boring; we get bored because our attention wanders. Giving someone our full attention says clearly, "You matter to me. You have my respect."

Attention is very much like a dog. Some years ago my friend Steve acquired a large, affectionate, and utterly blithe-spirited retriever pup whom his son named Ganesha. Ganesha had a lot of energy, and he had never been trained; he was accustomed to doing whatever he liked. If you put him in the yard, he would dig under the fence. Leave him in the bedroom and he would chew up your slippers. Take him for a walk and in a minute he would be halfway across a field chasing a deer. So Steve started to train him. For a while, I thought it was the other way around: Ganesha would bark and then Steve would run after him. But now, after a lot of patient practice, Ganesha has learned to heel and to expend his energy on a fast run at the beach instead of on bedroom slippers.

Attention can be trained in a very similar way. At first it wanders restlessly all over, looking into everything and everybody. But if we put it on a short leash and recall it many, many times, the great day will come when it will heel and obey. Then it becomes an alert, invaluable companion – very much like a well-trained sheep dog, which I have seen follow all kinds of complicated instructions. Over the years, I have come to the conclusion that there is no limit to the degree to which attention can be trained. That is how responsive it is.

Almost every disruption in human relationships – between parent and child, man and woman, friend and friend, worker and co-worker – can be prevented by learning control over attention; for with attention comes loyalty, interest, desire, trust. I can illustrate with the most fascinating of relationships: the romantic. Suppose *Romeo and Juliet* had turned out differently, and the two lovers had married and settled down to a normal domestic life. After a few years, as sometimes happens, Romeo's attention gets restless, and Juliet loses her attraction. Once the very sight of her made him think of flowers and bubbling brooks and the "light, sweet airs of spring"; now she just reminds him of the laundry and his morning espresso. Once he used to hang on her every word; now he answers everything with "Fine" and "Have a nice day." After a while his attention falls on Rosaline, his old flame.

Now *she* reminds him of flowers and brooks; his attention grabs onto her and will not let go.

If he could read what most of us read today, the advice he would get is, "Follow your desires. That is where happiness will be." That is just where unhappiness will be. If Romeo's attention cannot stay with Juliet, how is it going to stay with Rosaline? After all, Juliet is the same Juliet, no less attractive than before. But Romeo is also the same Romeo. If he cannot get control over his attention, happiness can only get farther and farther away.

The moment you hear the brook babbling and start thinking about spring, withdraw your attention completely from Rosaline and focus it on Juliet. With practice, we can focus our attention by choice just as intensely as it is focused by first love. Then Romeo will find that every day with Juliet is as sweet as the first. Every morning he will be able to exclaim with fresh wonder, "It is the east, and Juliet is the sun!" And the love between them will grow deeper and richer every day. As Teresa of Avila says, *"Amor saca amor"*: love draws out love.

Energy

To love, we have to be able to do things for others, even if it is inconvenient. We have to be able to do things we do not like even when we seem to have no willpower or energy. When we know we should help Johnny with his homework but have only enough energy to drop into a beanbag chair with a martini, one way of looking at the problem is that we are out of gas. Why? We eat good food, get enough sleep; we have plenty of energy for doing things we like. How can we get more energy, so that we can give more love?

When people ask me this, I usually point out, "You already have a lot of energy." As far as human beings are concerned, there is no real energy crisis. All of us have vast amounts of vitality. But we fritter it away, letting it flow out wastefully through one hundred and one channels.

Here again, there is a close connection with attention. Energy drains out when we let the mind go on working, repeating the same thought over and over. I have seen learned names for this phenomenon too, but I would compare it simply with a broken record. When a phonograph record becomes scratched, you know, the needle jumps the groove and keeps repeating the same few words or notes. The mind jumps its grooves too. It begins playing one of its little tunes – "Roses are red, violets are blue, Tchaikovsky is great and so are you" – and all of a sudden it is "Tchaikovsky, Tchaikovsky, Tchaikovsky . . ." That is all that most guilt complexes amount to, most compulsive memories, most resentments, most obsessions: sitting there like the little dog listening obediently to "His Master's Voice" while the same old thought goes round and round and round. There is no serious mental malady here, only a minor mechanical problem.

When we know how to meditate well, if the mind slips into a negative groove, we can lift it up gently and set it down on something positive.

This is not turning away from problems or playing Pollyanna. It is simply good energy conservation. Whatever problems we might have, dwelling on them is only going to magnify them, and waste a lot of time and energy in the process.

To put it another way, negative thoughts such as anger, resentment, greed, and worry are like holes in a tank, through which vitality drains. A few weeks ago, as we were driving to San Francisco, a car passed us leaving a trail of gasoline. About half an hour later we saw the same car parked on the shoulder of the road, out of gas. That is just what most of us do with the mind. It is full of energy, yet we go through life trying to punch as many holes in it as possible, multiplying our desires, our possessions, our anxieties, our frustrations until by the end of the day we have scarcely any energy left at all. The biggest of these holes is selfish desire. Thérèse of Lisieux was once asked by her older sister why she, Celine, was not making faster progress on the spiritual path. Thérèse took Celine's thumb and wrote on it playfully, "Too many desires." Vitality leaks out through every selfish desire. The more we want for ourselves, the less energy we shall have, and therefore the less capacity for love.

When we find it difficult to love other people or to put them first, we can think of it as a personal energy crisis. I read a lot today about the crisis with fossil fuels.

Many people still talk as if the only solution is to find some other source of power, but that is not enough; it is equally necessary to reduce consumption. The same is true when we are talking about our personal energy, our vitality. Here we have no atoms to split or fuse, no windmills to make, no sun to draw on for an alternative source of energy; we have to conserve what we have and make it last.

If we lived in a house with only one big battery's worth of electricity, we would be turning off lights right and left. If we had just one tank of fuel oil or gas, we would always be ready to turn down the heat. Similarly, when we are not using the mind, we can learn to turn it off. When some fierce desire is prompting us into action, we can learn to turn off the heat. The power is not lost. Instead of being wasted, it is consolidated as tremendous reserves of vitality, security, and self-mastery.

In today's consumer world, a lot of power is wasted in producing items which are neither necessary nor beneficial. But buying less and owning less conserves personal energy as well. Shopping for things we do not need, for example, wastes a lot of vitality, even if it is only window shopping; energy flows out with every little desire. It is a surprising connection, but an extravagant shopper will find it difficult to love. When such a person goes shopping, he or she scatters love like largesse all over the department store basement. We can become bankrupt in love this way, just as we can in money. So if you want a good, stiff test of your capacity to love, go into your favorite store some day – preferably when there is a sale – and see if you can walk straight through, looking neither left nor right, and come out unscathed. It may sound impossible, but it *can* be done.

Discrimination

This brings us to the fourth essential of love: the capacity to discriminate between right and wrong desires. The criteria are simple. Right desires benefit everyone – including, of course, ourselves. Wrong desires may be very pleasing, but they benefit no one – again, not even ourselves. The problem that arises is that wrong desires can be very skillful impersonators. They put on a three-piece suit and a false mustache and present themselves suavely as Mr. Right, the benefactor of all; if they happen to be just what we like, that is only a happy coincidence. To love, we need to be able to recognize right desires and yield to them, which is a pleasant but rare state of affairs. But much more importantly, we need to be able to recognize wrong desires and resist them, which is very, very difficult.

Again, I can give a small example from my own life. This morning my friend Laurel prepared especially for me some waffles made with finely ground almonds. They were not only a delicious, loving gift; they were also nutritious. So when she came to the door I welcomed the whole combination with open arms – her, the waffles, and my mind's desire to eat them. On the other hand, if I had come to the kitchen and found a package of frozen waffles lying on the table with a note saying, "I have to go to my golf lesson. Just pop these in the toaster according to the directions on the package" – well, if I *had* had a desire for waffles I would have told that desire, "Please stay out. I don't want to eat these; I don't want to see them; I don't even want to hear about them."

Most wrong desires, I admit, are not so easily resisted. We have to draw on every militant instinct we have to take on the desire person to person. We don't even know we have this choice. When a big desire comes, we think we have to yield. There is some pleasure in yielding; but if I may say so, there is much more lasting satisfaction in resisting, even if at first we do not win. The very attitude of resisting wrong desires is the beginning of good health, vitality, and love.

Not only that, resisting wrong desires actually generates energy. Whenever we can defy a powerful, selfish desire, immense power is released into our hands. I do not think this is even suspected outside the major religions of the world, yet it is the secret of all spiritual work and transformation.

Our desires are not our business alone; they are everybody's business. Whenever we resist a selfish desire, even if we do so for no one in particular, that is an act of love – just as every time we yield to a selfish desire, it shows want of love. The reason is simple: everything we do affects others, whether directly, through the environment, or by the force of our example. To me, for instance, smoking shows lack of love. First, the capacity for love is actually caught in that compulsion. But more than that, the smoke is harmful for everyone, and the example tells even casual passers-by, "Don't worry about the surgeon general. Don't worry about consequences; don't even think about the future. If it feels good, do it!"

Pelé, the great Brazilian soccer player, has long been in a position to command a king's ransom for endorsing commercial products. He has never given his endorsement to any brand of cigarettes, and I was very pleased to hear him give the reason in simple English: "I love kids." That is a perfect choice of words. He *does* love kids. He knows that in most of the world they will buy anything with his name on it. Therefore, though he came from a very poor family, no amount of money can tempt him to do something that will mislead young people or injure their health. To love is to be responsible like this in everything: the work we do, the things we buy, the food we eat, the people we look up to, the movies we see, the words we use, every choice we make from morning till night. That is the real measure of love; it is a wonderfully demanding responsibility.

Awareness of Unity

Discrimination, then, leads us naturally to the last quality for love: the awareness that life is one indivisible whole. This is the very basis of love. Any violation of the unity of life, whether it is between individuals, between nations, between us and the environment, or between us and our fellow creatures, is a failure of love. Everything that separates diminishes love; everything that unifies increases it. Lack of love divides; wealth of love heals.

To take just one aspect of this, you may recall Mother Teresa's brilliant truism: "It is always people you meet everywhere." Beneath the thinnest shell of differences, every one of us is very much the same, whether we live in Asia, Africa, Antarctica, or America. In times of nationalism or of international tension we forget this; if we remembered, no nation would ever go to war.

Once we realize the unity of life, we see the whole planet as a single family, whose welfare is indivisible. Most of us would not dream of tearing up our front yard, filling our garage with garbage, burning the porches for fuel, spraying noxious chemicals around the house, and then telling our children, "We're moving out. You can have whatever is left." That is exactly how we should feel about the earth. When we love all life as our family, it will be impossible for us to waste anything. We will want to share whatever we have – air, water, oil, food – not only with those who are alive today but with the children of the future, all of whom are our own.

Learning to love is not a luxury. It is a vital necessity – especially perhaps today, when the whole world, threatened with violence on every side, is starving for love and unity. "In the home," Mother Teresa says, "begins the disruption of the peace of the world." Similarly, it is in the home that the peace of the world is preserved. In nourishing our family, our community, and finally our world with love, turning our backs on ourselves when necessary to give what the world so desperately needs, we become, in the words of Saint Francis, instruments of peace.

Introduction by Carol Lee Flinders

All we know of Saint Paul is what we are told in the Acts of the Apostles, and what he tells us himself in his letters to the small communities of new Christians he had founded in cities like Corinth, Thessalonica, and Rome. Put every scrap of information together and you still have a very incomplete picture. It is incomplete by modern standards – we have no physical description, for example – but telling, all the same.

The turning point in Paul's life – the part of the story everyone has heard – is that on his way to Damascus, armed with letters from the high priest in Jerusalem which authorized the arrest of any Christians he could locate, he was struck down by a blinding light (it was or was not perceived by his companions, depending on which account you read) and heard a voice that said, "Saul, Saul, why dost thou persecute me? . . . I am Jesus whom thou persecutest." Saul asks what the Lord would have him do. "Arise," he is told, "and go into the city, and it shall be told thee what thou must do."

So began the heroic ministry of the Apostle Paul and the dissemination of the Gospel throughout the Gentile world.

If this were all we knew of Paul's conversion, the whole

train of events would seem disturbingly arbitrary. "The Lord works in mysterious ways," of course. But was there nothing in Saul's character that would help us make sense of such a radical change?

In fact, we do know more.

We know, to begin with, that Saul was a brilliant young man. He must have been, for he had had the privilege of studying with the greatest rabbi of the time, Gamaliel. We know that his family had attained Roman citizenship, which wasn't easy for Jews at that time.

We know, moreover, that he was passionately religious. By his lights, his foremost duty to the God of Israel was to root out the pernicious new faith by whatever means were at hand. He was fully prepared to live by those lights. "As for Saul, he made havoc of the church, entering into every house, and haling men and women committed them to prison." He was a man obsessed, his consciousness unified around a single purpose.

I have mentioned that one of the basic disciplines that Easwaran prescribes as a sure way to deepen one's meditation is the art of one-pointedness. By way of explaining its function, he has always insisted that the capacity to throw oneself heart and soul into something – tennis, ballet, politics, woodcarving – is in itself a sign of aptitude for the spiritual life, no matter how unlikely the individual might appear or how worldly the activity of choice.

Concentration, Easwaran believes, is the key to genius in any field, because when we can withdraw all our attention from everything except the one object or question or challenge at hand, we get access to inner resources that are normally locked away out of reach. In this sense, even a powerful emotion like anger or desire, when it unifies our attention completely, can open a door into deeper consciousness. The account of Saul's embarking for

Damascus — "breathing out threatenings and slaughter against the disciples of the Lord" — suggests that he was in just such a state.

What had stirred him to such a depth?

Just a few days before, Saul had been witness to an event of enormous significance in the history of early Christianity: the stoning to death of Stephen, its first martyr. Stephen had been preaching the Gospel to powerful effect — so powerful that his antagonists charged him with blasphemy and brought him before the high priest. Instead of refuting the charge, Stephen recounted the history of the Jews since the time of Abraham, and in the telling, he identified himself with the prophets who foretold the coming of the Messiah and his persecutors with those who had resisted the Holy Ghost. Frenzied, the crowd "gnashed on him with their teeth." Stephen was unaffected. "Being full of the Holy Ghost, they looked up steadfastly into heaven, and saw the glory of God, and Jesus standing on the right hand of God." He said as much, and his hearers "stopped their ears, and ran upon him with one accord; and cast him out of the city, and stoned him."

There is an expression to describe someone who does not join in an assault, but who stands by and tacitly supports it: "He held his coat." This is almost literally what Saul did in Stephen's case. "The witnesses laid down their clothes at a young man's feet, whose name was Saul. And they stoned Stephen. . . . And Saul was consenting unto his death." Whether Saul was present when Stephen addressed the crowd in the synagogue, whether he too "saw his face as it had been an angel," we don't know. But there can be no doubt that he saw him at the moment of his death and heard him "calling upon God, and saying, 'Lord Jesus, receive my spirit,'" and finally, "'Lord, lay not this sin to their charge.'" Stephen falls dead at the feet of Saul. Like a young lion who has tasted blood, Saul hurls himself into the pursuit of Stephen's fellow Christians. But it is no good. Something has happened to him, and within days he is brought down himself. "Trembling and astonished," he receives his orders: "Arise and go into the city, and it shall be told thee what thou must do."

Quite without Saul's awareness, something was transmitted at the moment of Stephen's death: a seed, or — more appropriately, to borrow the metaphor Easwaran uses in such instances — a depth charge, equipped with a delaying device so that the explosion in consciousness takes place days or weeks later.

What happened to Paul was dramatic — of cataclysmic proportion. But it bears on the lives of every one of us insofar as it is the prototype of something that, in a much less astonishing way, happens all the time — and not just to saints or martyrs.

Any man or woman who hopes to leave the world a more habitable place for their having passed through has reason to reflect at some point upon the enormous disparity between the ranged Powers That Be and the apparent powerlessness of the single, well-meaning individual.

History refutes this disparity, teaching us again and again, through the lives of great reformers like Mahatma Gandhi and Martin Luther King Jr., like Teresa of Avila and Catherine of Siena and John Woolman and many, many others, that the dedicated individual is in fact immensely powerful. Study their lives, see how many minor miracles had to take place to bring their work to fruition, and you begin to see that latent in human affairs, ambient in the very atmosphere — slumbering in every one of us — there is tremendous power for good: the moral equivalent of atomic power, and just as ubiquitous.

Gandhi never tired of bearing witness to that power. In 1946, when an American journalist asked, "How can we prevent the next war?" Gandhi replied: "By doing the right thing irrespective of what the world will do. Each individual must act according to his ability without waiting for others, if he wants to move them to act. There comes a time when an individual becomes irresistible and his action becomes all-pervasive in its effect. This comes when he reduces himself to zero."

Easwaran has a phrase to describe the strange magic by which the bottomless wellsprings of love, courage, and resourcefulness in all of us can be tapped. He speaks of a "stirring of the unconscious." Look deep into the eyes of a man or woman who knows what he or she is about and something in you stirs — rises up out of long sleep to answer them, just as it did in young Saul. When the Bible speaks of "bearing witness," then, words are not at issue. The real aim is the kindling by one individual in another of their divine potential: "deep calling unto deep."

Another way of putting this is to say that our real nature, yours and mine and everyone's, is love. Whatever other gifts we may have, we are at our most effective when we let ourselves act out of love. No one has conveyed this with more conviction and eloquence than Saint Paul himself, in the passage that follows — a perfect one for use in meditation.

Though I speak with the tongues of men and of angels, and have not love, I am become as sounding brass, or a tinkling cymbal. And though I have the gift of prophecy, and understand all mysteries, and all knowledge; and though I have all faith, so that I could remove mountains, and have not love, I am nothing. And though I bestow all my goods to feed the poor, and though I give my body to be burned, and have not love, it profiteth me nothing.

Love suffereth long, and is kind; love envieth not; love vaunteth not itself, is not puffed up; doth not behave itself unseemly; seeketh not her own, is not easily provoked, thinketh no evil; rejoiceth not in iniquity, but rejoiceth in the truth; beareth all things, believeth all things, hopeth all things, endureth all things.

Love never faileth: but whether there be prophesies, they shall fail; whether there be tongues, they shall cease; whether there be knowledge, it shall vanish away. For we know in part, and we prophesy in part. But when that which is perfect is come, then that which is in part shall be done away.

When I was a child, I spake as a child, I understood as a child: but when I became a man, I put away childish things. For now we see through a glass, darkly; but then face to face: now I know in part; but then shall I know even as also I am known.

And now abideth faith, hope, love, these three; but the greatest of these is love.

I CORINTHIANS 13

Epistle on Love

[1]

Saint Paul's "epistle on love" (I Corinthians 13) is an eloquent, practical little manual for loving, so pregnant with meaning that I recommend it to everyone for use in meditation. Some will prefer the King James Version, with its elevated beauty of language. Others will find that the words of a contemporary translation speak to them more directly. It does not matter; this is a personal choice. What is important is to translate Saint Paul's words into our thought and action, and for that purpose I want to comment on this masterpiece of Christian mysticism almost line by line to show its application to daily living.

"Earnestly desire the higher gifts" of the spirit, Paul begins, "and I will show you a more excellent way." The way of love is perfectly suited to our times. Instead of telling friends you are leading the spiritual life, which sometimes makes people raise their eyebrows, you can say, "I'm learning to love." It is the same. "He who loves not knows not God," Saint John says; "for God is love."

Learning to love in this way is the most difficult, the most demanding, the most delightful, and the most daring of disciplines. It does not mean loving only two or three members of your family; that can often be a kind of ego-annex. It does not mean loving only those who share your views, read the same newspapers, or play the same sports. Love, as Jesus puts it, means blessing those that curse you, doing good to those that hate you; that is the real measure of love. Of course, words like these describe great lovers of God. But little people like us can learn to love like this too. The first condition is simple: we must want to love. Desire is the basis of all learning.

In the style of his Master, Paul is asking, "Do you want to love – not just those who like you but even those who dislike you, the very sight of whom sends you hurrying in another direction?" All of us, I think, would like to answer yes. All of us really want to love. Nobody wants to be hostile, angry, or afraid, and all these states arise from lack of love. But we do not know how to love; and perhaps we do not even know that love can be learned.

Here Mother Teresa has given us a practical clue. Universal love, she points out, is first learned in the home. The family is our primary school for love, for it is within the circle of the family that we see ourselves most easily as part of a larger whole. When sociologists say that the days of the family are numbered, this is like saying that the days of our love are numbered. To love is to live, and not to love is to have nothing to live for.

Once we earnestly desire to learn this, we start to school in love. Most of us do not begin by blessing those that curse us. That is graduate school. We start with first grade – being kind to people in our family when they get resentful. Eventually comes high school, where we learn to move closer to those who are trying to shut themselves off from us. College means returning good will for ill will. Then we are no longer simply mastering words and behavior; we are actually changing the way we think. And finally we enter graduate school: "Return love for hatred." There we learn to give our love to all – to people of different races, different countries, different religions, different outlooks, different strata of society, without any sense of distinction or difference.

Paul, I must say, can really strike hard. His words are utterly contemporary. "I may have all the knowledge in the world," he says. "I may be able to speak fourteen languages, including one or two that are spoken only by angels. I may have crossed the Atlantic in a canoe with only a cat for company. What does it matter? If I haven't learned to love, I am nothing."

Here we have an authentic standard for the worth of our lives, the value of our times. Paul is asking, "How much are you worth?" If we reply airily, "Oh, about five hundred thousand dollars," he won't bat an eyelid. "I'm not asking about your bank account," he'll say. "I'm asking what you are worth."

"Well," we tell ourselves, "after all, this Paul comes from Asia Minor. Probably he doesn't understand English idioms, or maybe this is some kind of Greek pun." But Paul is being literal. We are conditioned to think of value in terms of money; it scarcely occurs to us that "what are you worth?" has nothing to do with money at all.

When we measure people and situations in terms of money, values become secondary. To give just one example, take a man who manufactures and sells weapons – or, for that matter, one who manufactures or advertises cigarettes, ignoring all the evidence about what smoking does to health. He may rent a Santa Claus suit at Christmas and fill stockings with gifts to express his affection, but Paul would still say, "He doesn't know how to love." When he learns, he will not be able to make money through activities that bring suffering to other people or other creatures.

The more we measure life in money, the less room there is for love. To show how far this can go, every day we read in the papers or hear from a neighbor that somebody's house has been broken into or somebody's wallet "lifted." The root cause of this kind of crime is our obsession with money and material possessions, which we ourselves have fostered – in our entertainment, our advertisements, our whole way of living. If we really desire to reverse this trend, we have to stop measuring people in money and start measuring them in love. If a woman has a million dollars in the bank, there is no connection with the kind of person she is. Instead of asking how much she has, we should ask, "How much does she give?" How much of her time does she give to others? How much of her work goes to benefit others? Only then do we begin to measure her real worth.

Again, take the business of moonlighting. I never learned this word in India, you know. When I first heard it in this country, I naturally assumed it was something romantic. But moonlighting is the opposite of romantic when its purpose is just to provide more "discretionary income." Instead of bringing people together, it can actually divide them. You want a second car so you don't have to share the first; then your partner wants another TV so you can each watch the program of your choice. Finally you are down to dual toasters, his and hers. When this happens, you are actually moving apart. Of course, there are extreme situations when a person has to hold two jobs. But the vast majority of us show our love much better if we give our time and energy to our families instead of taking a second job to buy them more things.

Somebody who loves easily, who can turn his back when necessary on personal profit or pleasure, is rich in love, a real tycoon in tenderness. Conversely, somebody who thinks only about himself — who can't think about the fellow next door or the family from the other side of the tracks, who can't identify with people from another race or country or color – that person is a skinflint. He won't give a tender thought to anybody.

At the University of California, Berkeley, there is a hill overlooking a beautiful outdoor theater. When I was there in the sixties, if Howlin' Wolf came to the Greek Theatre, graduate students whose stipends had run out or freshmen who had blown their remittance at the pizza parlor would creep up to watch from Tightwad Hill, where without a ticket they could make out Mr. Wolf's silhouette and occasionally hear him howl. This is a compassionate way to look at people who cannot think about others – they watch life from Tightwad Hill. But at the same time, it shows that by their own token they are not worth much. After all – at least in the days when I was there – it took only five dollars to go to the Greek Theatre. To go instead to Tightwad Hill, you have to be either the flintiest of skinflints or utterly down-and-out.

Here, I think, it is good to give people a wide margin of understanding, especially when they are young. In India, where families often make severe sacrifices to send a son or daughter to college, everyone is patient with a student who is out of cash. If you are waiting in line for tickets with two or three friends, for example, and your turn comes at the box office window, everyone understands if you suddenly discover that your shoelace has come loose. You bend down to tie it, giving your friends a chance to buy your ticket, and everybody knows there is no question of generosity or stinginess; you simply do not have the capacity to pay. Similarly, when someone suddenly gets angry, you can think to yourself, "Well, his shoelace has just come untied." Whatever he was doing before, he has to bend down and look at his feet; he hasn't got attention to give to anything else. When a person can't think about anything except himself, all he has time for in life is tying shoelaces; after two or three steps they are undone again.

The truly wealthy person, on the other hand, is one who has a genius for not thinking about himself. He or she simply forgets to ask questions like "How does this affect my feelings?" When I was in Berkeley, it was impossible to pass a pizza parlor or coffeehouse without finding two people intimately discussing each other's subconscious. A great lover has a genius for not thinking about his subconscious. All his sensitiveness is opened out to those around him.

Such people have a genius for happiness as well. They don't get offended because they are not brooding on themselves. Similarly, they don't get upset. If you are unkind to them, they can oppose you kindly – not because they feel hurt, but because they understand the damage your ill will does to you. If you insult them, they will feel sorry for you; you are exposing yourself as a miser.

If we could only realize it, all of us are billionaires in love. Our inner resources are infinite. By keeping the doors to this interior treasury closed, we have learned to live like paupers, sometimes even bankrupting our lives and the lives of those around us. Most of the conditions of modern life which we decry and suffer from today, particularly the sharp rise in violence and crime, have not been imported from some other planet. We ourselves have made our society what it is; we have made our world what it is. But there is a very positive side to this: if we have done all these things, we can undo them also. By drawing on our vast capacity for love, every one of us can make a lasting contribution to world peace.

In this sense, Saint Paul's Epistle is a detailed, practical guide for "profiting from a financial crisis," which will tell us not how to get more from life but how to give more – how to make ourselves rich in love.

[2]

Love suffereth long, and is kind; love envieth not; love vaunteth not itself, is not puffed up; doth not behave itself unseemly.

My grandmother was fond of a Sanskrit saying: "Patience is the ornament of the brave." Patience, not retaliation, is the real badge of courage. I would add, patience is equally the mark of love.

To be a good teacher, you need patience. To excel in anything you have to have patience. But if you want to love – which means, in my language, if you want to live – patience is an absolute necessity. You may be dashing, glamorous, fascinating, and alluring; you may be tall, dark, and handsome, lissome, lovely, and conversing with a tape recorder about cigarettes and cigars, so I returned the cassette to the library. But if I had persisted all the way to Lesson 52, I am sure I would be reading the *Interior Castle* in Spanish and reciting lines from John of the Cross in a good Castilian accent. That is the purpose of such courses: you do Lesson 1, then Lesson 2, and fifty-two lessons later you speak Spanish. Of course, these methods are not flawless. I remember a cartoon showing a man and his wife in a European restaurant staring at a big platter on the table in front of them, on which there is a sewing machine covered with spaghetti. The wife is saying, "I *told* you not to try to order in Italian!" Self-help has its hazards, but by and large, if you do your lessons diligently and keep on plodding, you will reach your goal.

It is exactly the same with patience. If you find somebody irritating, don't avoid that person; you would be missing a precious educational opportunity. Being with people is an essential part of the course. Most of us, when we see someone exasperating coming up our front steps, want to get into the closet, pull an overcoat in front of us, and call out, "There's no one home!" If you really want to learn patience, however, you will say, "Great! This is Lesson 10 in the course," and open the door with a smile.

On the Blue Mountain, my wife and I had a good friend who had come to India from England as a missionary and later joined Mahatma Gandhi. One of this lady's frequent visitors was an acquaintance with such difficult ways that the very sight of her was enough to elevate our friend's blood pressure. One day she asked me, "What should I do? Should I hide when I see her coming and refuse to answer the door?"

"No, no," I said. "Just repeat the Holy Name – *Jesus, Jesus, Jesus.*"

After a week or so she came to me again. "It's no use," she said. "Once I hear that particular knock, my mind gets agitated before I even think of Jesus."

I got a good idea. "Make it a race," I suggested. "The moment you see her turn in at the gate, start the name of Jesus going. See if it can get into your consciousness before she reaches the door."

Our friend kept at it with British bulldog persistence. I never asked how the race was going, but one day I was pleased to hear her announce, "Oh, by the way, do you remember my friend so-and-so? I don't get agitated around her any more. When I see her coming up the walk, the Holy Name dashes along next to her and beats her to the door."

This is one of the simplest ways of learning to be patient. When irritation calls and demands an immediate answer, the Holy Name puts it on hold, giving the mind a few precious minutes to prepare itself so that it can push the harsh words back. In other words, the Holy Name gives us a chance to respond to events the way we choose.

There is a close connection between speed and impatience. Impatience is simply the mind being in a hurry; that is why one of the steps in my eight-point program is slowing down. Our culture has become so speeded-up today that we scarcely have an opportunity to learn to be patient; everyone is in too much of a hurry. People in a hurry cannot be patient. People in a hurry cannot love. To love you need to be sensitive to those around you, which is impossible if you are always racing through life engrossed in all the things you need to do before sunset. In fact, I would go to the extent of saying that a latecomer will find it difficult to love; he will be in too much of a hurry. A late riser will find it difficult to love; she will be going through the day trying to catch up.

Of course, it is easy to be patient when people agree with you. It becomes difficult when others criticize you or contradict you or do not do what you want. This kind of contrariness is part of life. If all five and a half billion of us thought and spoke and acted alike, the world would be about as interesting as a condominium with every room the same. Fortunately, we come from different homes, went to different schools, hold different jobs, have been exposed to different influences. Naturally, when we get together in close relationships, we differ in all kinds of ways, some of them not very pleasant. If we are going to love, we have to accept difficult relationships; that is life. But this is not a matter for resignation. When you love, you live among difficulties not with resignation but with rejoicing.

The secret of this is profoundly simple: these differences amount to no more than one percent of who we are. Ninety-nine percent is what we have in common.

percent you. Being with people who are different is not only unavoidable; it is a precious, vital necessity. Without the company of those who differ from us, we grow rigid and narrow-minded. Those who associate only with people their own age, for example, lose a great deal: the young have much to learn from the old, and older people from the young. Similarly, if you are a blue-collar worker, it is good to know an intellectual with a Ph.D. or two; it will cure you of any awe you might have of experts. If you are a university graduate, there is no reason to stop speaking to your high school friends who went straight into work. Even the difference between an egghead and a hardhat is only one percent. Their feelings, their responses to life's perennial problems, are very much the same.

Most disagreements, in other words, do not really go very deep. They are not settled by arguing. They are not solved through analysis and synthesis. They are resolved, or dissolved, through patience. Without patience you start retaliating, and the other person gets more upset and retaliates too. Soon you have two people out of control. Instead, listen to what the other person is saying. How can you even answer if you do not listen? Repeat the Holy Name, refrain from answering immediately, and when you can, try a smile or a kind word; it can do so much to relax the atmosphere. Little by little you can try a kind phrase, then a kind sentence. When you become really expert in love, you can throw in a kind subordinate clause.

This actually quiets the other person. Kind language is a sedative. When you answer harsh words or disrespect with kind words, you are writing a prescription and passing it to the other person: "Take this. It will keep your blood pressure down and calm your mind."

This is a vital skill, for whatever our role in life – student, teacher, doctor, parent, carpenter – we can't depend on people doing what we say in just the way we like. If you are a doctor, for example, you cannot expect to get patients who are well-behaved, courteous, and prepared to carry out instructions cheerfully. You are going to get many whiny children and irritable adults. You will see people who are short-tempered, ask embarrassing questions, demand to see your diploma, and wouldn't dream of following instructions they do not like. This is part of being a doctor. But every patient like that is a lesson in love. When the nurse comes in and says, "You've got a real pill this time, doctor," you can say, "Terrific! I'm getting a lot of lessons today; I'm going to learn patience fast." Maybe the patient hasn't slept. He has been in pain for forty-eight hours, hasn't been able to eat his breakfast; do you expect him to be an angel? If you can be patient with him, it may help as much as any medication. It is not only drugs or surgical procedures that help your patient. At least as important is the faith that you are not just doing a job for pay or for some personal research interest; you are concerned about his welfare.

"Love suffereth long and is kind," Saint Paul says.

There is a close connection; sometimes patience is the greatest part of being kind. This word "kind" is so simple that we seem to have forgotten what it means; it opens a great avenue of love. One medieval Western mystic asks, "Do you want to be a saint? Be kind, be kind, be kind." I would say, "If you want to be a great lover, be kind, kind everywhere, kind to all."

This is the rub. Most of us can be kind under certain circumstances – at the right time, with the right people, in a certain place. Otherwise we simply stay away. We avoid someone, change jobs, leave home; if we have to, we move to southern California. But as Jesus says, being kind when it is easy to be kind is not worthy of much applause. If we want to be kind always, we have to move closer to difficult people instead of moving away.

Thérèse of Lisieux, a charming saint of nineteenth-century France who died in her early twenties, was a great artist at this. In her convent there was a senior nun whose manner Thérèse found offensive in every way. Like many of her sister nuns, I imagine, all that she wanted was to avoid this unfortunate woman. But Thérèse had daring. Where everyone else would slip away, she began to go out of her way to see this woman who made her skin crawl. She would speak kindly to her, sometimes bring her flowers, give her her best smile, and in general "do everything for her that I would do for someone I most love." Because of this love, the woman began to get secure and to respond.

One day, in one of the most memorable scenes in Thérèse's autobiography, this other nun goes to Thérèse and asks, "Tell me, Sister, what is it about me that you find so appealing? You have such love in your smile when you see me, and your eyes shine with happiness." Her very image of herself has changed; for the first time in her life, perhaps, she has begun to think, "I must be a lovable woman!" That is the healing power of kindness, which we should never forget even though we are so seldom able to observe it. "Oh!" Thérèse writes. "How could I tell her that it was Jesus I loved in her — Jesus who makes sweet that which is most bitter."

In every disagreement, I would say — not only in the home but even at the international level — it is really not ideological differences that divide people. It is lack of respect, which I would call lack of love. Most disagreements do not even require dialogue; all that is necessary is a set of flash cards. If Romeo wants to make a point with Juliet, he may have elaborate intellectual arguments for buttressing his case, but while his mouth is talking away, his hand just brings out a big card and shows it to Juliet's face: "I'm right." Then Juliet flashes one of hers: "You're wrong!" You can use the same cards for all occasions, because that is all most quarrels amount to.

What provokes people in a quarrel is not so much facts or opinions, but the arrogance of these flash cards. Kindness here means the generous admission — not only with the tongue but with the heart — that there is something in what you say, just as there is something in what I say. If I can listen to you with respect, it is usually only a short time before you listen with respect to me. Once this attitude is established, most differences can be made up. It may require a lot of hard work, but the problem is no longer insoluble.

When two people quarrel, they take for granted that they are adversaries. That very attitude is the problem between them, not the difference of opinion. We think that a quarrel has to have a right side and a wrong, a winner and a loser. With this attitude, both sides are losers. The problem is not solved; at best it is simply terminated. The difficulty is in the way the lines are drawn: "This is you against me." It is not; it is you and me against the problem. To resolve our differences, I have to push the problem over to the other side and pull you over to my side; then we can plan together to solve the problem. After all, we have a common goal: how to resolve that problem to the satisfaction of both sides.

"Love envieth not; love vaunteth not itself, is not puffed up." There is a common element here. Our usual idea is that when love is intense, jealousy has to creep in. Saint Paul is reminding us that when love is present, jealousy *cannot* creep in. Similarly, when jealousy is present, there is no room for love; we are thinking of ourselves. And everything is distorted. You see some little thing – a remark, a look, a handkerchief in someone else's possession – and you brood on it, make up all kinds of fanciful explanations, put two and two together and get twenty-two. Jealous people do not see what is there; they see what jealousy puts there. And then, tragically, they start thinking and acting as if all this were true.

In village festivals in India, we have a version of the "old shell game" that is played with three coconut shells. The showman says, "Put your rupee down, friends! I'm going to show you just where I put this ball. Place your rupee near that shell. If the ball is still there when I lift the shell up, I'll give you ten rupees back!" He shows everyone the ball, then lifts one of the coconut shells, puts the ball into it, and returns it to its place. "You saw me do it," he says. "If you believe your own eyes, why not put your money down?"

Somehow there is always a surprising number of villagers to say, "How simple! Instead of working all day, why not accept this foolish fellow's invitation? After all, I have sharp eyes. I saw where he put the ball." One by one, they put their money down. Some hold back; but as their neighbors step forward they say, "Well, if Raman is going to go home nine rupees richer, why shouldn't I?"

The man allows some time for all this; he even lets people arrange to borrow. Then he raises the coconut shell – and there is no ball.

I could have wept every time this happened, especially when I saw the look on those villagers' faces. Most of them didn't have a rupee to lose. And they just couldn't believe their eyes. "We *saw* it there!" They were all so sure.

Anyone who knows even a little about magic knows that the ball was never placed under the shell. It goes back into the man's palm. That is just what happens in jealousy. "I saw this. I saw him. I saw her. I saw them." What did you see? Jealousy is a great magician; insecurity is a house of mirrors. Saint Paul reminds us, "Love trusts all things." Where there is jealousy, we *cannot* see clearly. Even if it develops that there is some reason to be jealous, I would still say trust people. Trust those you love. Most people will respond.

There is another side of jealousy, and that is competition. Competition, as the British economist E. F. Schumacher says, is usually no more than jealousy and greed. You want something that somebody else has, or something you think somebody else has. Whether you need it is irrelevant. If Jack or Martha has it, you feel inferior unless you can have it too. Without comparing yourself with Jack or Martha, of course, this cannot happen. When I hear talk about "keeping up with the Joneses," I ask, "Who are these Joneses?" Keep up with your Self – with the spark of divinity within you. Let the Joneses keep up with their Self.

Jealousy can be so meaningless! Whatever assets you may have, if you are jealous, you will not be able to see those assets or give them their real worth. All you will see is something you do not have, compared with which your assets amount to nothing.

Fortunately, freedom from jealousy can be obtained by everybody. All that is required is to stop comparing yourself with others, which is one of the marvelous applications of training attention. Jealousy comes from insecurity. The answer to jealousy, therefore, is not to acquire other things or to prove yourself superior to other people, but to move closer to people around you and make yourself more secure. The more secure you are, the less jealous you will be. On the other hand, the more you move away from others and compare yourself with them, the more jealous you have to be.

"Love is not boastful," insists Saint Paul. "It is not arrogant or rude." This too is a matter of attitude. The same lack of security that makes us feel inferior to some people can make us feel superior and behave with arrogance to others. We may not go around blowing our own trumpet, but we can be boastful in a much subtler, more insidious way. When we are angry, we are being boastful. When we deprecate someone, we are being boastful. Insecure people often get a dubious satisfaction in finding fault with others like this. Instead, Paul would say, why not support them and try to help them correct their faults? Whenever you find someone who is not as skillful as you are, or as efficient, or as secure, instead of criticizing or comparing, the best service you can render is to help and support. If it is necessary to oppose or correct that person, you can always do so with sympathy, kindness, and respect.

As you practice these skills of love – patience, kindness, not being arrogant, not being rude – your capacity for them will grow. In whatever field of service you have chosen, your influence will expand. "Blessed are the peacemakers," Jesus said, "for they shall be called children of God." We can all be peacemakers. We may start in a very small place – the home, the office – but gradually we may find ourselves in situations where we can make a lasting contribution to the safety of our neighborhood or the welfare of the world.

This is not an exaggeration. Every one of us is concerned about the threat of war today, when armed conflict even between small nations on the other side of the globe can plunge us all into nuclear disaster. I still remember vividly the words of President Kennedy: "If we do not put an end to war, war is going to put an end to us."

When we are angry in our home, we are conducting a little war. In European history, you may remember, there is the Thirty Years War. In the home it is only a Thirty Minutes War, but these conflicts have their consequences too, which extend beyond the walls; we take them with us wherever we go. We may have guerrilla warfare in the kitchen. I have seen Cold War on the same block. Personal resentments, personal hostility, lack of courtesy, lack of respect for others: the sum of all this, the mystics tell us, is what erupts into international war. War, we should all remember, does not come about through forces of nature. It is made, declared, waged, and continued by men and women like you and me.

Conflict and disharmony, in other words, are not only problems of personal relationships. National decisions too are made by individuals. It is not uncommon to see the government of one country behave with arrogance towards other countries, even other races; and the problems that result are very much the same, only vastly more dangerous. Similarly, the frightful arms races in which so many countries are caught today – fueled, I am sorry to say, by sales from the United States – is defended throughout the world as a matter of national security. I would not hesitate to say this is national insecurity, the most dangerous kind I can imagine. And this business of retaliation – "You did this to me, so I am going to do that to you" – has brought us frequently to the brink of world war.

Love has an essential, practical place in all human affairs, even among nations. It shows itself not in exploitation but in cooperation, in a readiness to look upon all countries as members of the same human family on the same very limited planet. With the threat and danger of global war growing precipitously, we cannot afford any longer to emphasize the one percent of differences among nations. We need to do everything possible to apply the way of love even at an international level: to approach other countries with respect, pursue mutual understanding with tireless patience, keep our eyes resolutely on what we have in common with other nations rather than on our differences, and above all remember that no country on earth faces a more disastrous problem and maple syrup. You come to the breakfast table rubbing your hands in anticipation. "Where are those pancakes? I'm famished!" And your partner says, "Guess what? I've made Belgian waffles this morning, just for you."

If you have strong likes and dislikes, your jaw drops; you sit down like a martyr. "Why couldn't you have made Belgian *pancakes?*" This kind of question can really hurt.

"That's not what Belgium is famous for," your partner says. "It's waffles. Belgian waffles."

That is the time to start changing. The great lover looks up bravely, rubs his hands together with gusto, and says, "Bring them on!" You pour on a lot of maple syrup to drown every trace of Belgian waffle, and then you really go through the pile. "These are good!" you can say. "If I'd known they'd be like this, I wouldn't even have mentioned blueberry pancakes."

It is the same at work. Most of us have our little quirks about how we approach a job, and about how we do it too. Josephine, say, likes to put her file folders in the cabinet sideways. That is how she has always done it, so she finds her system very easy to use. If you want to increase friction, you can insist on your own way. But if you want to love, listen to your co-workers patiently; respect their ways. When you have to correct someone, you can always do so kindly and respectfully.

This is not at all easy; it can even be grueling. But like an athlete in training, you are training for love.

Love, like any skill, is learned through incessant practice. As Saint Francis de Sales says, we learn to speak by speaking; we learn to run by running. And we learn to love by loving; there is no other way.

After training all day you are exhausted, and so is your partner. When you come home in the evening, all you want is to be left alone. "After all," you say, "haven't I earned it?" Unfortunately, this is like a marathon runner coming home from her workout and saying, "Wow, I really ran hard today! I deserve a three-scoop sundae." Just like her, you're still in training.

The tennis finals are on tonight. You have your own TV in your bedroom, and every cell in your body is crying out, "Why not? Lock yourself in, set yourself down with a can of something that made Milwaukee famous, and just let your mind go with the match." But there is a knocking at the front door – your little boy's friend from across the street. "Hi!" he says. "Billy said you could help us tonight with our square roots."

Square roots! You thought you had heard the last of them twenty-five years ago. Haven't you paid your dues? "I'm sorry," you want to say. "I've been adding up figures for eight hours today and I've had it. The U.S. Open is on tonight and I intend to watch it." But then you catch the look in Billy's eyes, and you make yourself smile. "Okay," you say. "Tell me again what a square root is, and I will help you find some."

To me this shows great love. You may think you are only relearning mathematics that night, but in fact you are doing something much more important: you are learning to love, and by your example you are teaching those children how to love too.

"Love does not insist on its own way." This does not mean never doing something we enjoy. But Saint Paul asks, "Why not widen the circle of what you enjoy?" Instead of enjoying only the things we like, we can teach ourselves to enjoy things that other people like as well – our partner, our children, our friends.

This is a marvelous capacity. The Plaza, say, has been building up to a Beatles festival all month long. For one night only, you can sit through hours of the Beatles and recall the good old days. Naturally, you have been keeping that evening open ever since you saw the billing. But since you're not sure what your family will think about it, you haven't mentioned your plans.

The great night arrives; tunes have been running through your mind all day. At the dinner table, you clear your throat. "Ahem! What would you all think of a movie tonight?"

"Oh, dad! How did you know?" Little Jeanie has the movie page of the paper right by the chair. She has been taking ballet lessons this year, and tonight – how wonderful! – the Bijou has Baryshnikov in a film version of *Swan Lake*.

Your heart drops into your shoes. You can't make head or tail of ballet; you can't even say Baryshnikov's name. And you've been looking forward for so long to Paul McCartney and his friends! But you can see how much it means to Jeanie, so you force yourself to get up and smile. And you go and sit cheerfully through the whole thing. You don't just close your eyes and sleep, either. You don't pretend to watch while drifting off into a world of fantasy, recalling *Yellow Submarine*. You watch Baryshnikov through Jeanie's eyes, giving the performance your best attention and trying to understand what it is that captures her imagination. In that very exercise you are showing love.

Afterwards Jeanie's ballet teacher comes up with her eyes glowing. "I've never seen anyone watch ballet with more attention! You must be a great lover of the arts." She peers at you more closely. "Perhaps you have even studied at the Bolshoi in your younger years."

"Actually," you reply apologetically, "it's Jeanie who loves it. But I love Jeanie, so I am going to learn to love it too."

Of course, you have to use your discrimination. If Jeanie wants to see *Friday the 13th Part XXXIII,* you don't say, "Well, I love you, so I'll learn to enjoy watching mayhem and mutilation right along with you." You say, "I love you, so I'll take you to *The Black Stallion* instead." There is room for a good deal of artistry in this. You know the great harm that violence in the media does, especially to young people. But on the other hand, you don't just say, "I forbid you to go!" Instead, you harness Jeanie's moviegoing desire to a better alternative: a good film, a really entertaining play, a special outing, something she will enjoy but which stimulates sensitivity, sympathy, or understanding.

For people who have difficulties in loving, this is one of the surest ways to train. It applies not only to a family; you can do it with your friends also. Those who are really daring can even take out an enemy or two. It's a splendid opportunity. Pick out someone you really dislike and say, "I've got two tickets for *Best of Enemies* tonight; why don't you come along?" If you think it is hard to concentrate on Baryshnikov with your little girl at your side, just see what happens when Mr. Grump is there instead! Your attention will wander continuously, flickering from the screen to your animosity. Your mind will beg, "Let me be anywhere else!" By facing obstacles like this, love grows by leaps and bounds. Just keep repeating the Holy Name and concentrate on the screen; you will see how much power the Name can generate.

Many years ago, when my mother was still living with us here in California, a friend of ours decided to amuse her by bringing a tiny frog. She placed it on the table, and I was startled to see it hop once or twice in a lethargic sort of way. Since she was a pediatrician, I thought perhaps she had brought in a frog with anemia. Then I noticed that she had a little switch in her hand; when she pressed the switch, the toy would leap.

My mother was not particularly impressed.

Coming from a small Indian village, she thought it strange that a full-fledged physician should be playing with an electric frog. But I exclaimed, "That's just what the Holy Name can do!" It is a kind of mental power switch. Every time you use it, you get a little jump. If you keep on repeating it, you can jump right over an obstacle in the way of love.

Actually, the Holy Name has a much closer connection with medical practice than that frog. Violated self-will can cause a lot of physical problems. Most people are aware that stress can be terribly harmful on the body, but few realize how much emotional stress comes from inflated self-will. We insist on our own way, and when we do not get it, we blow up – in anger, frustration or insidious chronic resentment, all of which in the long run damage the vital organs severely. Love is essential not only for emotional health but for physical well-being too; kindness and patience are excellent preventive medicine.

People who have very little self-will don't much mind being contradicted. They have enough patience to say, "Well, if it releases some of your tension to blow up at me, go ahead." This is a particularly daring kind of love. The interesting thing is that when people find they cannot provoke you, they often do not keep trying. Usually they become quite decent when they are with you; they reserve their irascibility for someone they can provoke instead.

"Love," says Paul, "is not easily provoked, thinketh no evil." Being irritable and being resentful both come from self-will. If you have pronounced likes and dislikes, which is the manifold expression of self-will, irritation and resentment will be your constant companions. There will be things or people to irritate you throughout the day.

This can be seen even among great artists, where likes and dislikes are often virulent. There is a famous hotel in London, the Savoy, which used to attract some of the best-known actors, actresses, and literary figures around. One English actor was so particular about his room at the Savoy that when he arrived, everything in the room had to be exactly the way it was when he left, even if he had last been there a year ago and was only going to stay for a few days. To him it was his room, and if so much as a cup was on a different corner of the table, he would get insecure and raise a fuss. The management, of course, found tactful ways of dealing with such difficulties. When this great artist left, the hotel staff photographed his room meticulously; then they went ahead and rented it to someone else. When they heard that he was returning, they would take out the photographs and rearrange everything to match.

Many of us behave this way. We may not be so transparent about it, but we too have to have everything in the "right" place – that is, the way we like it. This goes not only for things but for other people. Our friend George is expected to talk this way; if he does not, we get irritated. Suzy is not expected to act that way; if she does, we feel resentful. Instead of trying to get people to keep changing with our moods, which is not likely to be successful, Saint Paul suggests, "Why not make yourself secure?" Let people change their attitude if they like; let the management change the furniture. Why should that affect our security or undermine our love?

A vague sense of irritation is so common today that many of us scarcely notice it. Virtually no one is exempt. We may not be able to pin it on any cause or refer it to any particular person, but some days there is a general sense of dissatisfaction which is just waiting to break into anger. When you sit down to breakfast or walk into the office, it is as if your mind is looking around like a hawk and saying, "What's going to irritate me today?" That is the time to be especially vigilant. Usually we feel it is the other person's job to be vigilant. "Watch out! I'm in a bad mood today. I got up on the wrong side of the bed; so I am forced to say something rude to the first person I see, and you are it." In all fairness, it is we who should watch out. What happens in our minds is our business to control.

For this kind of vague, subclinical irritation – what Dr. Friedman calls "free-floating hostility" – the Holy Name can be very effective. When a baby is crying and the mother needs to finish her work, she sometimes puts a pacifier between the baby's lips and it satisfies him for a while. The Holy Name is a pacifier for grown-ups. When you feel irritable, just put it between your lips and keep it there – *Jesus, Jesus, Jesus,* or whatever it may be. When the irritation is gone, you can take the Holy Name out.

Resentment and irritation come easily when the mind wanders, which it always will until it is trained. Resentment, for example, is a common burden on those who like to live in the past. It is essentially because we are not completely here in the present that a part of our attention gets caught in the library of the past. Like a graduate student at the university, attention has a cramped carrel in this library, piled with musty memories. If the print is small, the mind studies it with a magnifying glass until one minor incident fills the field of vision. And of course there are tapes to listen to; if the memory is faint, the mind has a dial that can take the little remark Suzanne made last summer and amplify and replay it to our heart's content. The mind gets caught; it has wandered in and now it cannot leave.

When I went to the shoe store with some children the other day, they all came out with balloons, most of which exploded in the car. But one survived; its owner held it very carefully between his hands and kept gazing at it admiringly. When we reached home, where the other children had only bedraggled-looking pieces of rubber, this boy's balloon even seemed to have swelled in size.

That is what we do with resentment: we take a memory, dwell on it, and inflate it with our attention. In the end it becomes like one of the huge traveling balloons we used to see in the skies above Sonoma County, in which for a handsome sum you could have a champagne breakfast on the prevailing air currents and perhaps enjoy the thrill of landing in a haystack or drifting out to sea. Resentment, however, offers no champagne. All we are served is a big breakfast of negative feelings.

Here, too, the answer is the Holy Name. If you keep on using it, the big balloon of resentment that can sweep you so far from reality begins to shrink until it is too small to lift even your pet poodle. Finally it bursts, just as those of our children did in the car. When this happened, of course, the children cried. But we adults can laugh when a resentment bursts; so much of a burden falls away!

"Love rejoiceth not in iniquity, but rejoiceth in the truth." When we are thinking about ourselves, it can be very difficult to see clearly what is right and what is wrong. One of the simplest ways is to ask whether what we are planning is for the good of the whole – our family, our neighborhood, our globe – or only for our own benefit or interest. Love, says Paul, cannot be private; it cannot be exclusive. It enjoys what is good for all, in which the good of each individual is included.

"When I was a child, I spake as a child, I understood as a child, I thought as a child; but when I became a man, I put away childish things." I was watching children in nursery school the other day. When they do not get their way, it is their prerogative to cry; it is their privilege. But a loving parent will have enough detachment to see that letting children have their way all the time will make life terribly difficult for them later on. Wherever you find adults having difficulty in listening to constructive criticism, the seeds of that difficulty were planted in early childhood. By not saying no, we can cripple a child for life.

This is a toddler's way of expressing disapproval — kicking his legs, upsetting his milk, and then lifting the roof. When we get older we say instead, "I'm not going to speak to him. When I see him coming, I'm going to look away." "I'm not going to work with her any more; I'm going to sit in my room and read *Gone with the Wind.*" When we do this, we are still children. To grow up, as Saint Paul says, we have to reduce self-will. That is the very essence of love. If you have to have your way, if you cannot go against your likes and dislikes for another person's sake, how can you love? At best you can have a kind of affection that comes and goes. Love does not ebb or fall; it is a continuing state of consciousness. When you love a person, you love that person always. Then the nexus of likes and dislikes is cut. You can want to see the Beatles all day long and when the choice with Baryshnikov comes up, there is no conflict; you can drop your preference effortlessly and find joy in your daughter's enjoyment.

This joy can be multiplied over and over. If there is such joy in loving one person, how much more is there in loving all! The more people we love, the greater our joy. When self-will vanishes and all barriers to love fall, we actually are in love with everyone; we have five and a half billion reasons for living.

[4]

For we know in part, and we prophesy in part. But when that which is perfect is come, then that which is in part shall be done away.

In his infinite love, the Lord has drawn a curtain between us and what may come. When my friends Laurel and Ed were designing a calendar, they worried for a while about what holidays to print in the boxes. They had to include Christmas and Hanukkah and Yom Kippur, of course, but how about Ramadan and Krishna Jayanti? How about Secretaries' Day and Gandhi's birthday? To put things in perspective, I suggested, "Suppose you could make a calendar showing everything that would happen in the coming year." We would be afraid to get out of bed, you know.

My grandmother's attitude toward the future was very practical. "Why do you want to know?" she would ask. "If you learn to love, you can face the future under any circumstances." Today, after years of arduous practice, I have no anxiety whatever about the future, though with the work of our meditation center I share many heavy burdens. I understand now that if we live wisely and selflessly today, only good can come of it, whatever else the future may bring.

Time past and time future, to paraphrase T. S. Eliot,

are both contained in time present. Just as our situation today is the result of what we have thought, said, and done in the past, what we think, say, and do today is shaping our tomorrow. The future is not fixed; it is in our hands. Instead of getting extrasensory glimpses of something that may or may not happen, Paul says, isn't it much more important to live wisely here in the present? The future will take care of itself.

Similarly for this business of tongues. It is, I agree, useful and interesting to learn languages. Our University of California offers courses in more languages alive and dead than most mortals have ever heard of. But even if it offered "Tongues of the Angels 101," how would that help us to love? Whether or not we can talk with Saint Peter in the vernacular of heaven, he is still going to ask, "Have you learned to love? Do you insist on your own way? Can you be patient and kind?"

In Indian bazaars and marketplaces, street performers of all kinds try to attract attention with a fascinating patter. They know one or two sentences in each of about ten Indian languages, and before they start juggling or bring out their trained monkeys, they run through all these variations for the benefit of passersby from different parts of India. I used to enjoy listening to them very much. But after the patter was over I would walk away, because usually that was the best part of the performance.

Similarly, Paul says, you may know the word for love "in the language of men and of angels"; it will not help you to love. No kind of knowledge can serve much purpose in bringing about the transformation of character, conduct, and consciousness which love entails.

All of us who have been associated with colleges or universities know how many people travel around the world learning new languages or looking into old ones. The mystics tell us unanimously, "There is a first-priority task awaiting you at home." As Socrates puts it, "Know thyself." Jesus says, "Forget yourself." It is the same: to know our real Self, we have to forget our small, personal self, the ego. Until we do this, everything else can wait. It is not that it is unimportant to learn Ugaritic or translate Panini's grammar into Turkish. But first let us discover who we are and learn to love.

For there is not much time. Every Saturday evening I think to myself, "Another Saturday has come. Another week has gone." Do not ask for whom Saturday comes; it comes for thee. Every day when the sun rises and sets it should be a reminder to us: our lives too have risen; our lives too are going to set. There is an extraordinarily sensitive kind of human being for whom this realization goes like an arrow into the depths of consciousness. For such a person all other priorities gradually dwindle; the most urgent priority in life becomes the realization of God.

How much of our time is preoccupied with the future! To keep abreast of the fascinating tendencies of our times I look at a number of papers regularly, beginning in the morning with the *San Francisco Chroni-*

cle and the *New York Times.* Usually I concentrate on the news, but if Christine says, "This column is especially good today," I read that too. In the evening I get the *San Francisco Examiner,* and from the university campus I get the student perspective in the *Daily Californian.* And on weekends I make my way through the Sunday edition of the *New York Times,* which is mammoth, probably the biggest paper in the world. Quite a lot of the mammoth is ads.

What interests me is that most of this vast amount of paper is unnecessary. A few months ago, for example, you could have put thirty days worth of newspapers into one sentence: "Will so-and-so run again or not?" That was all anybody had to say. Instead of cutting down all those trees and running the presses overtime to bring out "tomorrow's news today," why not just send out a postcard? All this to look into the future! If you try to apply Paul's advice here, you will find there is very little to read. We have a pungent phrase in my mother tongue: *charvita-charvanam,* "chewing what has already been chewed." Once you have chewed it, why go on chewing over and over for thirty days?

"For our knowledge is imperfect," Saint Paul says, "and our prophecy is imperfect." This holds true for all human knowledge; it applies to a world that is constantly changing. Economics, for example, has absorbed human interest for thousands of years; yet as someone remarked recently, it is still in the Stone Age. My college economics professor, a good teacher, was candid with us from the very first day. "This is not a course in poetry or art," he warned. "Economics is called 'the dismal science.'" The more I studied it, the better I understood why. Nothing in it is certain. I think it is Truman who remarked that what the country needs is a one-handed economist: everything is always "On the one hand . . . but then, on the other . . ."

There is a story (probably apocryphal) about a maharaja in British India who went to the London School of Economics to study under Harold Laski. Laski was an institution; as Galbraith would say, he was "present at the Creation." For many influential people, what Laski said was law. This maharaja felt he had benefited so much from Laski's instruction that when his son came of age, he sent him to Laski too.

Naturally when the boy returned to India after his first year, his father was eager to hear what his former professor had learned in the twenty years since he had been his student. He asked his son, "What subjects did you have to write on for your exam?" The boy told him, and his father shook his head in disbelief. "The university must have become fossilized," he said sadly. "The great man has grown senile. Those are the very same questions he gave us when I was there." And he added, "When you go back, please give my regards to your professor and ask why he is still asking the same old questions."

The boy did as he was told. When he returned to his father again, it was with a terse reply from Laski:

"True, the questions are the same. But the answers have all changed."

It is the same in the not-so-dismal sciences. If you want to see the mutability of knowledge, open a textbook of medicine from just fifty years ago. You will find how many certainties have become ambiguities, how many cure-alls have become either cure-nothings or cause-alls. This does not reflect a flaw in medicine; change is the nature of knowledge. Similarly, I remember one of our own Berkeley astronomers making a public statement that took me by surprise. "We astronomers seem to have erred," he said, "in what we have been saying about this particular phenomenon."

"Really?" asked the reporters. "In what way?"

"It seems the truth is exactly the opposite of what we thought."

In contrast, no spiritual teacher has ever recommended impatience as the answer to insecurity. No scripture has ever said, "Get angry and be healthy" or "Be greedy and be loved." It is always the same old story, the same old timeless truths. When someone objects to me, "There is nothing new in what you are saying," I reply, "Of course not. That is why these truths are so valuable." What would Saint Paul's advice on love be worth if twenty years later he had to say, "Recent advances in the theory and practice of love have made it necessary to issue this revised edition"?

Similarly, love does not change. As Shakespeare says, "it is an ever-fixèd mark." By this criterion, love that comes and goes with fortune is not love. Shakespeare gives a memorable illustration of this in the character of Sir John Falstaff, a huge, boastful, outrageous, endearing old soldier. Young "Prince Hal," before he became King Henry V, did his share of painting the seamier side of London red, and he and Falstaff were close cronies. Despite his coarse nature Falstaff was a loving man with a loving heart, very fond of his friend Hal. When the prince is about to be crowned king of England, Falstaff is overjoyed. He goes about telling all his disreputable friends, "Whatever you want, just ask me. Do you want a position at the palace? Want to get into Parliament? Declare war against Finland? Just ask me; my Hal is going to be king." At the coronation, he rushes up with his unlikely crew to embrace his friend in front of all the courtiers and nobility. And King Henry, in one of the great scenes in Shakespeare, looks down at him and asks his court, "Who is this man? I know him not." When we next hear of Falstaff he is a broken man, who dies of a broken heart.

We are so physically oriented that we think this is dramatic metaphor. Dying in an automobile accident we can understand, but "dying of a broken heart"? It is not metaphor. Death from bereavement does not take place immediately, but loss of love takes away the will to live. Correspondingly, love brings life; love heals and makes whole. The more you love, the more reason you have to live. The more you love, the more precious your life will be to everyone around.

[5]

For now we see through a glass, darkly; but then face to face: now I know in part; but then shall I know even as also I am known.

I saw an advertisement the other day which said, "I like my real me. And my clothes show my real me." I wanted to object, "If that is your real you, it will be going to the cleaners once a week." We forget that clothes are just the covering; they are not the contents. Similarly, the body is just a covering. The face you see in the mirror is not your real face. Until you realize the Lord, Saint Paul would say, you have not seen your real face; you have not even seen the faces of those around you.

When we are angry, we are hiding our real face. When we are greedy or resentful or afraid, we are wearing a mask. Love means taking off all these masks. When we do this, we see the Lord in everyone – as Nicholas of Cusa says, "the Face behind all faces."

Our personality, in other words, is just a kind of makeup. Getting angry is like taking out a jar of red choleric face powder and smearing it around our eyes and mouth. Many people, I am told, put creams on their faces and then go to sleep in the hope of improving their complexion. One of the most remarkable recommendations I have heard of is avocado paste. It shows how easily we human beings can be taken in. Any sensible person would object, "Avocado paste is for making guacamole." It's not for the face; it's for eating with corn chips. Who knows? Someday we may be told that rubbing bing cherries around the eyes will give a permanent reddish tint that the covers of fashion magazines will extol. I don't know how much it helps to sleep with your eyes covered by guacamole or bing cherries, but if you fall asleep with anger makeup on, you are likely to wake up with crows-feet under the eyes. Even for physical beauty, we need to take off the makeup of anger.

Stage makeup can be so elaborate that it takes hours to put on. It also takes hours to get it off. Anger makeup is taken off by not getting angry. It may take years to remove it completely, but every bit that is taken off reveals a little more of our natural beauty. Once it is all off, we do not need to add any makeup for beauty. It is already there; our real face shines with love.

I wish you could look through my eyes at someone who is angry; you would never want to be angry again. I used to say this to the freshmen in my English classes, and it really went home. For some reason, if you tell people that anger is a thousandth of a heart attack, it may not have much of an effect. But if you say, "It makes your face look like a prune," everybody responds. You can see so many face-marring influences at work in anger; each little capillary announces, "I am not pretty." When we stop dwelling on ourselves, on the other hand, our skin and eyes and smile begin to shine with beauty.

When we see the Lord within us face to face, as Saint Paul puts it, we see simultaneously that the Lord shines from every face around us. In terms of physical knowledge – names, nationalities, hair colors, Social Security numbers – to know everyone would require many lives. But to understand others as they really are, all we have to do is know ourselves.

"But when that which is perfect is come, then that which is in part shall be done away." That is the key sentence. Jesus says, "Be ye perfect, even as your Father in heaven is perfect." It *is* possible to become perfect in love. In the fullness of love, all imperfections pass away. "Love is infallible," says William Law. "It has no errors, for all errors are the want of love."

This kind of love can never be broken, not even by time or death. It is a force which is not at all dependent on the physical body. If you love a particular person more than yourself, this force cannot be disrupted when the body dies. Every act and thought is a force in consciousness, and consciousness is not dissolved at death. Just as waves go on spreading long after a pebble is dropped into a lake, the force of love continues to operate.

Love becomes perfect when the mind is stilled and self-will ceases. Then we live in love always. Physically, of course, we still inhabit a body in San Francisco or

Saskatoon. But inwardly we live in a very different world, the Land of Love: as Teresa of Avila says, in the light that has no night.

I have to admit that I still enjoy travel literature. Most of the papers I read have weekly articles offering all sorts of enticements. You can travel by camel or kayak, paddle around with penguins on a raft in the Antarctic, even take courses while you go from place to place. This is horizontal travel, where you stay on the surface of life. But what I find much more fascinating is vertical travel. This is meditation, the whole purpose of which is to take us to the Land of Love in the utmost depths of consciousness.

For a long, long time we may not get very far on this journey. We may even spend a few years sitting in the foyer of the travel agency, falling asleep over the brochures. But a few insist on traveling deep. Then meditation ceases to be a dull, dreary discipline; it becomes a daring, even dangerous adventure. And once you look around beneath the surface, wanderlust gets whetted as on your first world cruise. It is like seeing Hawaii for the first time; everything seems absorbing: the leis, the coconut palms, the mangoes and papayas at every meal. "This is really interesting!" you say. "So different from Peoria!" Then you go to Australia, which is different still; each kangaroo and koala is captivating. As you go further the language changes; things become more difficult to understand. I remember passing through France on my first trip to this country from India. I might as well have been deaf. *Qu'est-ce que c'est?* was just sounds to me; I didn't even know it was a question. All this is very much like what happens in the depths of meditation as we move from one level of consciousness to another.

By and large, this development takes place in two ways. It may come on so quietly that you are scarcely aware of anything happening. But if you are meditating earnestly along the lines I recommend, it is more likely that very gradually, over a long period of time, you will become absorbed in the words of the passage. Concentration deepens, so that the words come more and more slowly. Then, perhaps for only a minute or two, the words dissolve in silence. But although they have disappeared, their meaning remains, very much as the fragrance remains after a vase of roses is taken from a room. When you return to the passage, you are in a different realm of consciousness. You don't understand the language. The words may just seem noises. But little by little, the way your eyes grow accustomed to the darkness when you enter a theater, you begin to understand where you are. In time you will learn to walk about in this new realm, to understand the sounds and sights and feel at home.

Over the years you pass through level after level like this, just the way one travels from one country to another, until finally you reach the very seabed of consciousness. This is the Land of Love. The whole personality is flooded with love, from the surface to

Introduction by Carol Lee Flinders

"Is not happiness precisely what all seek, so that there is not one who does not desire it?"

Most of us would answer this question, which Augustine asked himself in his *Confessions,* rather brusquely. "Everybody knows that. It's no more than a truism."

To take the truism one step further, wouldn't nearly every one of us accept readily that no matter which specific thing we may be pursuing at a given moment, it is joy, lasting joy, we are hoping against hope to turn it into? Yet for Augustine, even as a young man, this very question opened the door to further questions:

> But where did they know [happiness], that they should desire it so? Where have they seen it, that they should love it? Obviously we have it in some way, but I do not know how. Unless we knew the thing with certain knowledge, we could not will it with so certain a will. . . . May it be that one gets joy from this, one from that? One man may get it one way, another another, yet all alike are striving to attain this one thing, namely, that they may be joyful.

So began a line of inquiry, a search – for the thing "we have in some way, but I do not know how" – that was to last a lifetime. Not only that, this search was destined to engage, eventually, the leaders of the Christian Church at a most critical point in history.

Though Augustine's mother, Monica, sought to bring him up as a pious boy, his own passionate temperament took him down many of the byways familiar to every ordinary adolescent. Growing up in fourth-century Roman North Africa, he saw many traditions mingle – and clash. The backdrop was formed of the folkways of his native North Africa, which were usually termed "pagan." Against these loomed the orthodox traditions emanating from the Roman seat of empire, including a Christianity which young Augustine scrupulously avoided. Then from the Near East were spreading Manichean ideas, which found a place in the imagination especially of the young. Augustine's description of college life in Carthage strikes startlingly familiar chords in anyone who has spent time on a cosmopolitan campus. Fraternities of Eversores, which translates roughly as "upsetters," delighted in terrorizing students and teachers alike; to be one of them, Augustine notes, was "a notable way of being in fashion."

As part of his college syllabus Augustine read a book by Cicero, and the entire direction of his life was changed:

Suddenly all empty hope for my career lost its appeal, and I was left with an unbelievable fire in my heart, desiring the deathless qualities of Wisdom. I should not chase after this or that philosophical sect, but should love Wisdom, of whatever kind it should be.

Even more critical, perhaps, was his encounter in Milan with the bishop of that city, Ambrose. Augustine was a teacher of rhetoric, and it was Ambrose's brilliance in the pulpit that drew him to his services. But it was the content of those sermons that kept him there. For the first time, Augustine realized one could be an intellectual and a man of God at the same time.

One day someone told him the story of Anthony and the Desert Fathers, who had begun their own kind of experiment in Egypt not long before. Inside Augustine something cataclysmic burst; he turned to his companion and cried, "What is the matter with us? These men have none of our education, yet they stand up and storm the gates of heaven."

He took refuge in the garden. After a long bout of tumultuous conflict, he ended by demanding of himself, "How long shall I go on saying 'Tomorrow, tomorrow'? Why not make an end of my ugly sins at this moment?"

Weeping, reiterating his bitterly heartfelt questions, Augustine flung himself down under a fig tree. All at once he heard the voice of a child, singing what sounded like the refrain of a game: "Take it and read, take it and read." Take what? Read what? He was sure he knew. Seizing the book he had just been reading, the Epistles of Paul, he opened it and read: ". . . not in reveling and drunkenness, not in lust and wantonness, not in quarrels and rivalries. Rather arm yourselves with the Lord Jesus Christ, and spend no more thought on nature and nature's appetites."

The crisis was past; his path was clear. Augustine sought from Ambrose himself instruction in the mysteries of the catechism, was baptized, and soon set sail for North Africa again with two lifelong friends, to devote, as a monk, all his energies to his interior search.

Most Christians of that period held that the sincere desire to receive the grace of God, manifested in the act of baptism, ensured freedom from sin. Yet Augustine, given to unremitting self-examination, came to see very quickly that the simple desire to be free from sin was not nearly enough. "What temptations I can resist, and what I cannot, I know not," he confessed. He found himself far from being able to rest content with being "saved" in the abstract. He wanted a personal faith that could save him in reality, and a method by which he could painstakingly strive to perfect his human personality. It was in meditating profoundly on the words of Jesus and of Paul that he began to see his own shortcomings in stark relief. Then, methodically, in the style of a contemporary man in a desperate situation, he undertook the lifelong endeavor of confronting his own weaknesses face to face.

He ran directly into the obstacles all of us face. He calls these obstacles "chains of habit," the habits of mind, like self-centeredness and greed, that we all cultivate in our ignorance, which bind us to sinning as surely as iron shackles bind a prisoner. It is because of these mental habits that our intentions to do good, no matter how sincere, often have very little impact on our actions. He then set himself a series of critical questions: "How then can sin be overcome? Is there no free will in us, to do as we think best? How are we to approach a Good that has no substance?" In his *Confessions* he attempted to detail for us, much in the fashion of autobiographical self-revelation so popular today, his struggle to answer these doubts.

The *Confessions* is the first spiritual autobiography in the Western world. Augustine was a true pioneer in the depths of the human soul. He wrote as a guide, appealing to his own experience to illustrate the numberless twists and turns of the mind along the route towards the universal spark of divinity within. In analyzing himself, Augustine was analyzing all mankind. God's will, he concluded, cannot even be guessed at, let alone followed, till a man breaks away from the bonds of his own twisted will.

And I marveled to find that at last I loved you and not some phantom instead of you; and I did not hesitate to enjoy my God, but was ravished to you by your beauty. Yet soon was I torn away from you again by my own weight, and fell again with torment to lower things. Still, the memory of you remained with me and I knew without doubt that it was you to whom I should cleave; though I was not yet such as could cleave to you.

This passion is often termed "the communion of love." It has become, as Evelyn Underhill puts it, "the heart of the Catholic faith," and in Augustine it fueled a life of heroic action on many fronts. His sermons and pamphlets and books, founded as they are on solid sensibility, are the groundwork upon which great spiritual figures in later centuries — Saint Bernard of Clairvaux, Richard of St. Victor, Saint Thomas Aquinas, and others — built painstakingly, describing and classifying the Christian mystical tradition into stages and substages of contemplation until a marvelous edifice took shape. Their writings in turn guided people as diverse as the Italian reformer Catherine of Genoa, the mystic poet Dante, the Spanish crusader of the spirit Teresa of Avila, and even Martin Luther. All these and myriad others, each with his or her unique blend of rapture, literary expression, and heroic social action, nurtured what is most enduring in Western civilization, and in each we can hear distinct echoes of Augustine.

Yet Augustine had pressing work in his own lifetime. Christianity, despite its official sanction, was not popular in many areas of the Roman Empire. Moreover, there were currents within the church, the Donatists in particular, which threatened to tear it into bickering factions.

Finally, the Western world in Augustine's time was poised on the brink of chaos. Whole races of barbarians had settled within the Empire; Augustine knew it was only a matter of time before they overran it completely. There was no time for bickering if the Church was to survive with its spiritual heart intact. Augustine dared to envision the "followers after perfection" as shining beacons for a world growing dark, and did not want to see the unique and particular quality of Christian revelation compromised. He took upon himself the awesome task of defining, as precisely as possible, the nature of that revelation for future generations.

The example of his group of monastic friends at the cathedral in Hippo, a spiritual enclave in the very heart of society from which pastors and bishops went out to serve the people, proved vital. After the fall of Rome, monastics gradually established communities on the fringes of civilization. They cleared and planted tracts in the wilderness, creating stable centers around which settlers gathered. Their influence spread all over Europe. When other educational institutions had vanished, they played a critical role in keeping the best in the classical tradition alive. Over the following tumultuous six hundred years, these communities remained precious repositories of the Christian revelation. Augustine's writings, along with the New Testament, were their principal sources.

Augustine went a long way toward defining what it means to adhere to a life of impassioned faith while at the same time acting in this world with consummate balance, formed of sensibility and compassion. Just as his words were a raft for people throughout the Middle Ages, when whole cultures were succumbing to the tides of change, they can be a lifesaver for people like us too, who live near the culmination of a long Age of Reason — and are still searching for a joy that lasts. Here, in the beautiful passage from the *Confessions* (Book I x , Chapter 10) which follows, Augustine has handed us a road map to that longed-for land. Yet, inevitably, it is up to us to do our own walking: "Let them walk, let them walk, lest darkness overtake them."

Imagine if all the tumult of the body were to quiet
down, along with all our busy thoughts about earth, sea,
and air;

if this very world should stop, and the mind cease
thinking about itself, go beyond itself, and be quite still;

if all the fantasies that appear in dreams and imagination should cease, and there should be no speech, no sign:

Imagine if all things that are perishable grew still – for
if we listen they are saying, "We did not make ourselves;
he made us who abides forever" – imagine, then, that they
should say this and fall silent, listening to the voice of him
who made them and not to that of his creation;

so that we should hear not his word through the tongues
of men, nor the voice of angels, nor the clouds' thunder, nor
any symbol, but the very Self which in these things we love,
and strain beyond ourselves to attain a flash of that eternal
wisdom which abides above all things:

And imagine if that moment were to go on and on,
leaving behind all other sights and sounds but this one
vision which ravishes and absorbs and fixes the beholder in
joy; so that the rest of eternal life were like that moment of
illumination which leaves us breathless:

Would this not be what is bidden in scripture, "Enter
thou into the joy of thy lord"?

AUGUSTINE, CONFESSIONS IX:10

Entering into Joy

Imagine if all the tumult of the body were to quiet down, along with all our busy thoughts about earth, sea, and air. . . .

This is a vivid way of describing the throng of traffic in body and mind, between which there is a vital, intimate connection.

With its intricate networks of transport and communications, we can compare the body to a state. It has its major arteries or freeways, its vessels like state highways, its capillaries or county roads. Altogether every human body contains five thousand miles of roads in its cardiovascular system, and they are busy every minute. Goods are trucked in to local tissue communities in a steady stream, while waste products are carried back out in empty vans.

Our nervous system, our communication network, is even more elaborate. I should make it clear that when I talk about the nervous system, I mean more than the tissues enumerated in *Gray's Anatomy*. The nervous system is essentially a process. The brain and the rest of the anatomical nervous system are the physical components that enable this process to function in the body – in computer language, the hardware. But the software, the processes which determine how the physical hardware is used, is the mind. These are not two distinct systems, but two aspects of one: how our nervous system responds to the world reflects the processes of our mind.

In this sense, we can think of the nervous system as a great highway like U.S. 101, which travels the length of the West Coast. Highway 101 is a busy artery; in places it has several lanes for traffic in both directions, divided by a median strip with elaborate plantings. Instead of speeding cars, however, imagine flashing thoughts and emotional impulses. In fact, our internal freeway is much more crowded than Highway 101. In the nervous system it is always five o'clock on a Friday afternoon; every moment carries peak traffic.

Whenever I ride along 101 and gaze up at the exclusive homes on the hills above the maelstrom of speed and noise, I wonder, "Who would ever want to live *there?*" Who would want to lie in bed at midnight listening to the roar of trucks, the din of cars? Yet we scarcely seem to notice when the mind is like this, though the result is stress throughout the day and often into the night as well.

When driving at freeway speeds, we are expected to keep several car-lengths between us and the bumper of the vehicle in front. In the nervous system no such rules of thumb are taken seriously. Thought-traffic is frenzied, almost by definition. Yet if each thought could just keep its distance from the next, we would find our mental traffic much easier to control. That is what quieting the mind means. When you look down from your hillside home overlooking the freeway of the mind, the traffic looks like one long, continuous blur. A burst of anger, for example, appears to be a smooth, rational flow of thought. This is the effect that speed of thought has on our perception of the mind. But if we can get traffic to slow down, we can examine each thought individually and even make out the bumper stickers: "If You're Looking for Fun, Follow Me" or "I Maintain My Right to Blow My Stack." I see stickers like these on cars; the stickers on thoughts are no more rational.

Unlike the freeway, however, traffic in the nervous system usually moves in only one direction: toward what we like and away from what we dislike. Over millions of years of evolution, the nervous system has been conditioned to be attracted by what is pleasant and repelled by what is unpleasant. Here the human mind makes an evolutionary contribution of its own: it begins to label as "pleasant" or "unpleasant" not merely physical sensations, but everything in its experience. In every situation, in other words, our characteristic response is "I like this" or "I don't like that." We can rationalize our decisions any way we want; ultimately they come down to this: "I am going to do this because I like it"; "I'm not going to do that because I can't stand it." We may know all about inductive and deductive logic, yet the simple ventriloquism of likes and dislikes escapes us: we say we make decisions, and nobody is more deceived than we ourselves. Similarly, when I witness a quarrel, it doesn't usually strike me as two people trying to convince each other of the logic of their positions; it strikes me as two people trying to deceive each other. "This is what I like, so you ought to like it too." Where is the logic in that?

The more I understand of human personality, the more impressed I am by how deep likes and dislikes can go. The process starts from our earliest days. Listen to the protests of a child when you try to get him to do something he doesn't want to do, or when you try to deprive her of something on which she has set her heart! In a child this kind of behavior can be easily forgiven, but later on it becomes a terrible handicap. People who allow their likes and dislikes to grow rigid become paralyzed when things don't work out the way they want. Relationships become a source of constant turmoil. In every circumstance, having strong likes and dislikes means trouble; a lower level of likes and dislikes means less tension and better performance. I would go to the extent of predicting that when you have quieted your likes and dislikes, your performance will be better in every area of life.

❧

In particular, having fewer likes and dislikes provides immense protection from stress. This is a popular subject today. Courses in stress reduction and management are increasingly attractive, as more and more people learn what damage a stressful life can do. But there is a good deal of confusion, even disagreement among experts, as to what the word *stress* should mean; so it is important here to be clear. According to Dr. Hans Selye, the "father of stress research," stress is the body's nonspecific response to a real or perceived threat. "Nonspecific" means that defense mechanisms (such as the fight-or-flight reaction) are triggered all over the body – unlike, say, the response to a bee sting, which is usually specific to the area that has been stung. You can imagine the damage these mechanisms can do to the body's major organs when stress becomes chronic.

What provokes the stress response? Broadly, there are two kinds of stressors. One kind is environmental, physiological, physical; the other is psychological. Dr. Selye says:

Mental tensions, frustrations, insecurity, and aimlessness are among the most damaging stressors, and psychosomatic studies have shown how often they cause migraine headache, peptic ulcers, heart attacks, hypertension, mental disease, suicide, or just hopeless unhappiness.

It is important to realize that unlike physical agents and situations, these and similar stressors are not external. They are produced by our state of mind. Frustration is not caused by Aunt Susie, but by our response to Aunt Susie: after all, her friends at work might respond to the same Susie quite differently. Mental depression, a terrible stressor, is not caused by a situation like being out of work, but by our response to being out of work. No one enjoys not being able to find a job, but what destroys a person's spirit, saps vitality, and sometimes even undermines the will to survive is not the fact of unemployment but the mind that is thrown into depression.

This is a subtle but very important distinction. Wherever possible, it is good to avoid external sources of stress like pollution-laden air or living in the flight path of a busy airport. But we should realize that many other things in our lives which we perceive as stressful – such as our job, where challenges and change may confront us daily – may not actually be stressful in themselves. Often the stress comes from our response. It is a great mistake, therefore, to think of "managing" stress by changing jobs or avoiding any of life's legitimate challenges. Dr. Selye, in fact, emphasizes that we live in a world full of stressful situations, and to run away from stress is to run from life. But by changing our mental responses, we can learn to manage stress: not merely to survive it, but to flourish in it.

Mahatma Gandhi is a perfect example of this.

When I first went to see him in his ashram in Central India, I was in my twenties and just out of college. People came from all over the world to see Gandhi then, because India's independence movement was in full swing and making international news. But most of them had come to see Gandhi the political figure, the man who was freeing a nation without firing a shot. I wanted to see Gandhi the man.

When I arrived at the ashram, I was told Gandhi had been in high-level negotiations with Indian and British political leaders throughout the day. Tensions ran high on both sides in those years. Great Britain, in the throes of the Great Depression at home, was losing control of India, the jewel of its empire and its major source of revenue; and on the Indian side leaders were pulling in different directions on fundamental issues, each trying to pull Gandhi with him. He was in his sixties then; imprisonment and a fearful "fast unto death" had taken a serious toll on his health. I knew that his daily schedule called for him to get up before dawn, keep busy all day, and often not get to bed until midnight or later. Recalling all this in front of the door of his cottage, I expected to see him come out exhausted, with the cares of a nation blearing his eyes and bowing down his shoulders.

Instead the door opened suddenly and out came Gandhi with his famous toothless smile, his eyes sparkling and full of love, as relaxed as if he had been doing nothing more challenging than playing cards. He must have just cracked a joke, because the men and women who came out with him, these austere states-men and politicians, were laughing like children; somehow their burdens had been lifted too. The stress of that day hadn't touched him in the slightest. He strode off for his evening walk with the light, swift step of a teenager, beckoning to us visitors to follow, and I remember I almost had to run to keep up with him. Many years later, friends who had worked closely with Gandhi told me that in his sixties he had three times the energy that most of us have in our prime. Yet he worked without tension, even in the midst of trials and sorrow.

Today people look at Gandhi's example and mar-vel, "What an extraordinary man!" Gandhi himself would say just the opposite: "Oh, no. Very ordinary." To me that is his greatness, his real stature. If he had been born a spiritual prodigy, able to cope with stress as effortlessly as those children I used to see on televi-sion who could work huge square roots in their heads, what hope could he offer little people like us? It is pre-cisely because he began life as such an ordinary figure that his example holds unlimited promise. "I have not the shadow of a doubt," he assures us, "that every man and woman can achieve what I have, if he or she would make the same effort and cultivate the same hope and faith."

Today, to explain his secret, I often come back to a phrase he used: "an undivided singleness of mind." That is a revealing clue. A one-pointed mind is slow and sound, which gives it immense resilience under stress. With a mind like this, we always have a choice in how we respond to life around us.

Virtually all psychological stress, I would say, comes from the rush and hurry of a frantic mind, which jumps recklessly to unwarranted conclusions, rushes to judgments, and often is going too fast to see events and people as they truly are. Such a mind keeps the body under continual tension. It is constantly on the move, desiring, worrying, hoping, fearing, planning, defending, rehearsing, criticizing; it cannot stop or rest except in deep sleep, when the whole body, particularly the nervous system, heaves a sigh of great relief and tries to repair the damage of the day. Simply by slowing down the mind – the first purpose of meditation – much of this tension can be removed. Then we are free to respond to life's difficulties not as sources of stress but as challenges, which will draw out of us deeper resources than we ever suspected we had.

✐

"Anxiety" is a useful term psychologists have for a particularly elusive kind of stress-related problem. Anxiety is as nonspecific in the mind as stress is in the body: faced by one threatening event, such as the loss of a job or the death of someone we love, the mind responds with fear and self-doubt in every area of life, in every relationship. Increasingly too clinicians refer to "free-floating anxiety," which is not triggered by any particular kind of external event but persists from situation to situation, characteristically when the ego feels threatened.

Primary care physicians admit that much of their work these days is an attempt to help people deal with anxiety, even though many of them would agree that anxiety is not a medical problem – in other words, that it has no medical solution. They prescribe tranquilizers or refer to a growing array of therapies, but by and large they are quick to confess that they are at a loss and are treating symptoms because they cannot reach the cause.

In the language of mysticism, as long as there is a division in consciousness between "I like this" and "I don't like that," that division itself will breed stress. It will be a breeding ground for anxiety. Just as malarial mosquitoes flourish in stagnant, marshy pools, anxiety flourishes in divided minds. Augustine delineated this split in consciousness in unforgettable terms:

> Who would choose trouble and difficulty? In adversity I desire prosperity; in prosperity I fear adversity. Yet what middle place is there between the two, where one's life may be other than trial? There is sorrow and sorrow again in the prosperity of this world: sorrow from the fear of adversity, sorrow from the corruption of joy. There is sorrow in the adversity of this world, and a second sorrow and a third from the longing for prosperity, and because adversity itself is hard, and for fear that

endurance may break. Is not life on earth trial without intermission?

The key to anxiety, as to psychological stress in general, is this: it is not so much an event or circumstance that brings on an attack of anxiety; it is the significance we ascribe to that event, the way we interpret it in our own mind.

I remember a classic illustration of how the mind works in this regard, where a woman spending the weekend in a prominent hotel in New York was kept awake throughout the night by someone banging away on a piano in the suite next door. The next morning, tired and irritated beyond belief, she stormed into the manager's office and demanded, "How can you allow such a thing to happen? I'm holding you personally responsible!"

"But madam," the manager responded smoothly, "that suite is occupied by the great Paderewski. He must have been practicing for his concert tomorrow in Carnegie Hall. People will be paying a small fortune to hear him play for a couple of hours, and here you have been able to listen to him all night long."

"Paderewski! In that case, please let me keep the room after all." And the same woman who had spent a whole night fussing and fuming, tossing and turning in frustration, sat up the next night with her ear glued to the wall, listening in devoted delight.

The same event that triggers anxiety in one person may be shrugged off by a second and even prompt a deep, resourceful response in a third. Again I can offer Gandhi as an illustration. When Gandhi arrived in South Africa at the age of twenty-three, he was an utter failure: in fact, his only reason for being in South Africa was that he had been unable to make a go of it in India. He had left home with his spirit apparently crushed. And as soon as he arrives in South Africa, he is bullied and thrown off a train for wearing a colored skin in a first-class railway car. Thousands of Indians must have suffered this kind of humiliation. Most, I imagine, responded with anger, fear, and then resignation, carrying away a deep injury to their sense of worth. But Gandhi's response plunged him into the depths of his being, where he made a decision that took decades to bear full fruit: never to submit to injustice and never to use unjust means to win a cause. It could have been one of the most stressful experiences in his life. Instead, as he later told the American missionary John Mott, it was the "most creative."

When we feel threatened by someone, often the cause of our anxiety is not that person at all; the cause is our perception of that person. We are put under stress by our dislike. But we can slowly learn to change our perception of others, no matter how they act, and thereby free ourselves from this kind of stress. This is the longest, most drawn-out fight we will ever find in life. Yet in the long run, no one can escape this fight. Every one of us must someday wage this battle within ourselves, against our own selfish, violent judgments of other people. Anxiety is only the warning system, warning us that something destructive is at work within and that we ourselves are its victims.

⊕

Through meditation and the enthusiastic observance of its allied disciplines, such as slowing down and keeping the mind one-pointed through the day, we can learn to do something that sounds impossible: when thoughts are tailgating each other, we can slip into the flow of mental traffic, separate thoughts that have locked bumpers, and slowly squeeze ourselves in between. It sounds terribly daring – the kind of stunt for which professionals in the movies are paid fortunes. Yet most of us critically underestimate our strength. We can learn to step right in front of onrushing emotional impulses such as fury and little by little, inch by hard-won inch, start pushing them apart. This takes a lot of solid muscle, in the form of willpower; but just as with muscles, we can build up willpower with good, old-fashioned practice.

As you learn to do this, you will find to your immense surprise that there is not the slightest connection between another person's provocation and your response. There seemed to be a connection because of the rush of the mind: your perceptions were crowding and pushing on angry thoughts of response. Now that those thoughts have been separated, your perception of the other person's behavior has lost its compulsive force.

We all believe there is a causal connection between perception and response; that is why virtually everyone reacts to the provocation of others. But from my own hard-won experience, I can tell you that it is possible, by strengthening the muscles of the will, to push thoughts and impulses so far apart that if someone gets annoyed with you, you can be even more considerate than before; if someone speaks rudely, you can answer with kindness.

This is what living in freedom means, and it is essentially a matter of getting over rigid likes and dislikes. When this freedom is won, a good deal of the mind's rush-hour traffic subsides. There will be an occasional car on your internal freeways, running a useful errand. Now and then there may even be a well-tuned Harley-Davidson. But by and large, the freeways of body and mind will be amazingly quiet.

Before we can experience this kind of peace of mind, however, a lot of hard work needs to be done. We must find a "middle place," as Augustine puts it, between likes and dislikes: in practical language, a new vital track within the nervous system on which our energy can travel.

At present, as I said earlier, our internal freeway is set up only for one-way traffic, one-way responses, conditioned by our likes and dislikes. When we have to go against our dislikes or do something unpleasant for the sake of others, it is like driving the wrong way into a one-way street. All the traffic of the nervous system is against us, honking, dodging, and complaining bitterly. Very much the same thing occurs when we have to deny ourselves something we want: it is like stalling our car across two lanes of rush-hour traffic, a highly unpopular maneuver. In general, I would say that many psychosomatic ailments like allergy and asthma may be the result of going against a dense, one-way stream of traffic of likes and dislikes: the nervous system cannot brook it, and the body complains. But we can learn to open up traffic in both directions; and when we do, we can move in either direction freely. This gives us the freedom to choose our responses even in tense, difficult situations.

But this is not just a matter of removing a road-block or two. For practical purposes, half the mind's freeway has never been constructed; we have to lay down a whole new road. Many years of sustained, often frustrating effort must go into building this road, but you will be more than satisfied when you see where it can take you. At first the endeavor may not seem so difficult. The terrain is flat, so to speak, and if you encounter an obstacle, you can build a detour without much extra work or cost. At this stage of getting over likes and dislikes, you probably are not sacrificing anything you care about deeply. But as you proceed, you run into places where likes and dislikes have hardened into habit. These are sedimentary formations of self-will, which can stop spiritual enthusiasm cold. Most of us never attempt to climb over these petrified habits of mind or to go around them. They hem us in, limit our vision, and prescribe our action.

That is why Augustine speaks of habit as the main obstacle in the life of every human being. The enemy is our selfish conditioning: some of it imposed from the outside, by circumstances, by friends, by the media; some of it imposed by our own choices and behavior. In the long run this selfish conditioning saps our will, until we finally forget that we have the choice of fighting it. Augustine describes this process in a vivid passage in his *Confessions*:

> The enemy had control of my will, and from that had made a chain to bind me fast. From a twisted will, desire had grown; and when desire is given satisfaction, habit is forged. When habit passes unresisted, a compulsive urge sets in. By these close-set links I was held. . . .

Popular psychology and the mass media insist that we indulge our whims and desires – often, in the case of the media, for somebody else's financial gain. This is not a moral issue to me; it is a thoroughly practical one, and Augustine states the reasons concisely. Every time we give in to a whim, especially a whim that benefits nobody, our will is weakened a little. Gradually, giving in becomes a habit; habit becomes conditioning; and conditioning binds our responses hand and foot.

Giving in to a whim comes down to likes and dislikes again – "I like this, so I'll do it"; "I don't like that, so I'll avoid it." To me this is a rather unchallenging pastime. Enjoying meaningless little pleasures and avoiding unpleasant chores is all a matter of coasting downhill; no effort or will is required. Working through a monolithic habit of likes and dislikes, by contrast, is a tremendous challenge that draws out all kinds of hidden resources. When you try it, you feel very much as if you were tunneling through a mountain of solid rock.

In the hills of Sausalito just north of the Golden Gate Bridge is a tunnel, called the Rainbow Tunnel ever since someone painted a rainbow over the arched entrance, through which Highway 101 snakes on its way north. To get a highway for two-way traffic, we have to cut tunnels like this through our likes and dislikes. Each tunnel can take months of hard labor; sometimes we have to endure long periods of frustration. You keep on trying to tunnel through the mass of habit, defying old desires, and for a long time you find no evidence that anything is happening. Here an experienced guide can be of enormous support. "Just keep on tunneling," he or she assures you again and again. "If you don't give up, you're sure to break through eventually." And after months – sometimes, for a really big compulsion, even years – you finally see a ray of light coming through from the other side.

Most of us have grown so used to giving in to little desires that we forget the role of the will. When we neglect the will, as Augustine says, and allow a desire to get stronger and stronger, we may find that opportunities for satisfying that desire come our way with increasing frequency. If we look closely, however, we generally find that we have been going out of our way to find opportunities. If we could interview a strong desire, it would have a fascinating story to tell: "He's been chasing *me!* I don't have to do a thing." We may not think we have made a conscious decision to pursue a particular object of desire, but on the unconscious level, a desire is a decision. One very effective way to strengthen the will, therefore, is to be extremely vigilant about not letting ourselves be put into situations where we are likely to be swept away by our desire. "Lead us not into temptation" means precisely this: don't put yourself into situations where your will is in over its head.

As a young man, Augustine had all the desires any normal person has. That is why he can understand and sympathize with our difficulties and conflicts. His advice is practical. "I do not blame you, I do not criticize you," he once told his congregation, "if worldly life is what you love. You can love this life all you want, as long as you know what to choose." And, I would add, as long as you have the will with which to choose it. We need both: the discrimination to see what is best in the long run, and the will to make wise decisions when the pleasures of the moment present a more attractive alternative. When we have both these capabilities, all the innocent pleasures of life can be ours to enjoy. In other words, this is neither license nor a plea for asceticism; it is a plea for building up our will.

Strengthening the will by defying strong selfish desires requires a long, grueling fight. But for those who are daring, there comes a turning point: you discover that there is more satisfaction in defying a desire than in yielding to it. After I tasted this fierce satisfaction of self-mastery, my perspective on life changed dramatically. From then on, I understood that building up the will could work wonders; and I started in defying desires joyously.

The psychology of this is fascinating. You are taking the joy right out of the hands of the desire and holding it up as booty: "Now I have the joy without you!" Desire comes as a bully pointing a pistol at you and demanding your life's savings, and like Humphrey Bogart you just take the gun out of his hands. When you can do this, your entire frame of reference changes. Most of the pleasures of the world pale into insignificance. It is not that they are no longer pleasant, but your capacity for joy is no longer limited to a few pennies of sensory pleasure; it is immense beyond belief, beyond all bounds. We can throw all our capacity for rebellion into this kind of heroism, defying our conditioned dependence on trivial likes and dislikes. In doing this, we break out of a narrow world into a new realm of freedom.

Repeating the name of the Lord can be of enormous help in this. When the Holy Name is repeated it becomes like a jackhammer, rattling away at the wall of solid rock that is conditioning. The amount of rock you dislodge per hour is not of primary importance; what is important is the number of times you remember to use the Holy Name and the enthusiasm with which you repeat it. Put as much enthusiasm into it as you can muster. When you can recall the Holy Name in times of stress, you will be making much more progress than you realize.

With the Holy Name, of course, goes meditation. Daily meditation enables you to bore deep into the rock of a compulsive like or dislike and set charges of dynamite at strategic points. Once meditation reaches a certain depth, the words of an inspirational passage like the Prayer of Saint Francis – "Where there is hatred, let me sow love" – can be truly explosive. Gradually deep cracks in the structure of self-will appear. Then the name of the Lord can serve as the kind of loader I saw the other day repairing a county road: it comes and clears the rubble from those explosive charges, so that the work of laying your new road-bed can proceed.

ᕗ

> *Imagine if the very world should stop, and the mind cease thinking about itself, go beyond itself, and be quite still: if all the fantasies that appear in dreams and imagination should cease, and there be no speech, no sign. . . .*

This idea of a still mind is unfamiliar to almost all of us, even threatening. We have conditioned the mind to go up and down: when we get our way, the mind gets excited; when we cannot have our way, the mind sinks into depression. Nobody wants depression, but excitement is another matter; without it, we feel, life is not worth living. So we go after excitement, and after every wave of stimulation comes a trough of depression. If we could gain enough detachment to watch the mind at work, it would look like a seesaw on the playground.

This phenomenon is closely related to something that is fast becoming a way of life today: distraction. At bottom, the habit of distraction stems from a desire to keep the mind in turmoil all the time. During World War II there was a Berlin-Rome axis; this false belief about the mind is the propaganda of what we might call the mind-body axis. To be really alive, we feel, the mind has to be stimulated constantly.

I have teacher friends who complain that most children today have difficulty in concentrating; their attention span is very short. This is often a direct result of distractibility. In fairness, this is not usually the children's fault. Modern civilization sets a premium on distraction, and the mass media are in front of children's eyes and in their ears to tell them constantly, "Keep your mind jumping! If you don't, you'll get bored."

Meditation is particularly effective in undoing this habit the mind has developed, for what distracts it again is its likes and dislikes. We should be able to put the mind on any subject and keep it focused there without any effort or protest, whether it likes the subject or not. This is what I call expert driving: you start the mind out on your mental highway, glide smoothly up to fifty-five, and cruise along in the same lane without any weaving in and out. When you can do this, you make a most rewarding discovery: everything you do with attention becomes interesting. This one skill can banish boredom forever.

Likes and dislikes tend to be most pronounced in our attitudes towards other people. If we want to be free to respond in kindness, free to love, free to contribute to others' welfare, we have to work constantly to keep our mind from heaving up and down. Otherwise we cannot even know what people around us are like. All that we know, if I may paraphrase a distinguished neuroscientist, is our own nervous system. When we say "I don't like that person," what we really mean is, "This is what my nervous system is recording: If I try to work with him I get migraine; if I talk to him, I break out in a rash; if I have to spend a few hours in his company, I can't sleep at night." We are not saying anything at all about that person; we are talking about our own signs and symptoms.

Similarly, when someone insults us, it is helpful to remember that that person has not really seen us at all. He is busy reading an EEG in his own head, and the report he is getting is highly negative. Instead of erupting at him, we should be able to say to ourselves, "Poor fellow! His nervous system is showing a highly destructive pattern." When you can do this, you can remain comfortable and secure in the face of wilting criticism. All your sympathy will go out to the person who is being unkind. This is a direct result of a still mind, and it is the very basis of compassion. It means you will be able to return sympathy for ill will, love for hatred, as Jesus recommended.

Every time your nervous system is making EEG recordings under the prompting of dislikes, it is putting you under stress. When Jesus says "Bless them that curse you; do good to them that hate you," it is your own health and peace of mind he is trying to safeguard. Being consistently kind is the best way to make your nervous system strong, healthy, and resilient. The best health insurance in the world, fittingly enough, is love. The surest immunity against the bacilli of suspicion and hatred comes with compassion.

Our goal is the capacity never even to think ill of others. But this does not mean we should fail to oppose other people lovingly when necessary. When someone is making a mistake or acting unkindly, putting up tender opposition is often a demonstration of just how much we care. But it is essential to oppose kindly, without withdrawing personal support, and not for the purpose of getting something we want or having our own way. And we must be prepared for the other person's aggravation. Yet after his initial displeasure at having been opposed, every sensitive person will realize that it is because we care for him so much that we have planted ourselves squarely in his path. In the long run, this will add respect and depth to our relationship.

With someone you are allergic to, my granny had a direct, daring way of tunneling into dislikes: try sitting down next to that person and starting up a pleasant conversation. You do not need to stay long; five casual minutes will do. It is the effort that counts. It may be painful at the time, but miraculously, over time, you are likely to find your allergy subsiding – not only with regard to that particular person, but toward anybody who happens to be discourteous to you or who contradicts you. This is an answer to many emotional problems that are rampant today, which we normally recognize only when they show up in statistics like the divorce rate. This simple skill will improve your health, your vitality, and ultimately even your physical appearance; for the mind in turmoil takes away from the beauty of our face, the beauty of our movements, the beauty of our voice, the beauty of our life.

On the other hand, always making yourself the frame of reference – which is precisely what having strong likes and dislikes means – is like spending the day being thrown like a Frisbee between conflicts. By evening you will be more tense than before, and so exhausted that you cannot face the problems you have created for yourself. Instead of allowing the mind to spin its numberless wheels, it is in our own best interest to extend ourselves by working hard and giving as much time and energy as we can to other people. If you want a good friend, don't think about

One of the miracles of the Holy Name is that it can help prevent thoughts and actions from becoming compulsive, simply by keeping the mind gainfully employed. Anger is always compulsive. Nobody really wants to get angry or to be resentful; that is the nobility of the human being. We get resentful because we think we cannot help getting resentful, and that is where the repetition of the name of the Lord comes in.

The farther you progress, the more clearly you will see the effect that bouts of excitement and anger have on the mind. One tantrum because you didn't get your way can cause giant mudslides in your hard-won tunnels. Instead of spending every day digging deeper into the rock, you find yourself having to spend days, weeks, sometimes months clearing out the debris.

In one particularly wet winter in northern California, we had such torrential rains that the roadway on the north side of the Golden Gate Bridge was in danger of washing down the cliffs into picturesque San Francisco Bay. It would have taken months and a good deal of the state highway budget to construct a new highway through the solid rock. Instead, the state engineers decided to shore up the existing road. They drilled deep holes into the underlying bedrock, inserted steel beams, and filled the holes back up with cement. Now this part of the highway is actually a bridge over the unstable earth. The name of the Lord is like those steel beams, and we can insert it whenever our self-control starts to slip. The Lord is there supporting us; all we have to do is maintain contact with him. He can help us avoid the pitfalls of daily living, saving us time and energy which we can use for making further progress. And with him shoring us up, we can be sure there is no chance of suffering the acute embarrassment of landing in the Bay.

There are serious long-term consequences from repeated lapses too. We begin to think that perhaps we are not going to make it to the other side of the mountain after all, that we can never learn to deal with the particular problems we face. I believe it was Sir Richard Steele who, when asked how he spent his days, replied candidly, "In sinning and repenting." You do a lot of strenuous digging, then yield to some tantrum or temptation, and there you are, digging out the same old ground again. So whenever you feel your mind is beginning to slip, indicating an impending mudslide of self-will, that is the time to be immediately on the alert. Then it is that the name of the Lord can help shore up your will.

I understand from the newspapers that some of the oldest highways in this country, the throughways in and around the big Eastern metropolitan areas, are in critical need of repair, and no one knows where to find the necessary funds. This is bad news for commerce, but in the conditioned highways of the mind it is a happy state of affairs. When your like-and-dislike throughways are splitting open and grass is sprouting up in the cracks, don't give them any attention with which to repair themselves. Just let them crumble quietly.

꘠

Augustine is trying in these lines to help us understand why we need to train our senses and learn to harness negative emotions. On the basis of the evidence provided by some of the greatest of mystics, this arduous effort is an unavoidable part of spiritual growth. Teresa of Avila, by her own candid account, spent nearly twenty years in this kind of tunneling. None of us therefore need be surprised if our road too is uphill for a long, long time. Many years of hammering away at the massed inertia of sense-conditioning and mind-conditioning is our lot.

Yet all in all, it is not very helpful to look on difficult situations and difficult people as impediments. We can look on them as opportunities, our great helpers. Everybody has difficulties in life; nobody can manage to get around this valuable training period. It is largely when we are not able to view difficulties as opportunities for growth that they become insufferable. We can learn to see frustrating circumstances or annoying acquaintances as opportunities to contribute more, opportunities to grow and to help other people grow. Without serious obstacles, I am afraid, very few of us would ever grow up. This is the purpose of obstacles: to give us the skill and confidence to face even bigger, more formidable obstacles.

Whenever people live together or work together, it is only natural that there be a certain amount of friction. There is nothing surprising about this. But every time you find yourself in a situation where you are getting hot under the collar, you can use the Holy Name to push angry words apart and stick in their place the desire to stand firm, stay patient, and help the other person calm down. Look at the drama of it: your blood pressure is hitting the ceiling, your eyes are getting bloodshot, all your juices are flowing in the wrong direction. To be able to remain patient and come out with kind words at such a time is making a U-turn right on the anger freeway. I'm told this used to be called "doing a brodie," after someone who presumably lived to tell the tale. On a highway, doing a brodie is a death-defying act, but on the highways of the mind it is life-affirming. When your mind is racing along some emotional freeway at top speed, headed straight for disaster, I don't think anything in life can equal the thrill of learning to do a brodie on the spot and drive back calmly in the opposite direction. Everyone will stop to stare and say in admiration, "Right on the freeway!" And after a while, everyone who sees you will want to learn how to do this too.

⊸

Often what prevents us from going against likes and dislikes in daily living is the enormous amount of mental furniture we keep. People can be very particular, you know, about how their household furniture is arranged. "My velveteen armchair goes here, a foot and a half to the left of the brass floor lamp. And my abstract acrylic sculpture has to sit on the far right-hand corner of the inlaid mahogany coffee table." We get used to a particular arrangement, and anything that disturbs it disturbs us as well. This is how we arrange the likes and dislikes in our mind too, and it limits us severely in our capacity to communicate with others and draw closer to them. The person whose mind is not crammed with likes and dislikes, whose taste in mental furniture is more in the "minimalist" mode, can go into any circle of people from any walk of life and communicate beautifully. He or she can rearrange the furniture of the mind effortlessly, as the situation demands; yet the resulting configuration will always be practical and beautiful. Teresa of Avila puts it plainly: "To have courage for whatever comes in life – everything lies in that."

Once we correct our perception of life around us, freeing it from the context of "I like" and "I don't like," all events are just events. They are neither pro nor con; they do not work for us or against us. The only thing we lose in this change of perception is our mental turmoil; for when you see everything as it is, you find there is no cause for personal sorrow. You gain compassion, you gain precious insight into others, and you gain the capacity to help them see more clearly, provided they want to see.

This does not take away from the joy of life; it brings added joy. When I take my friends out, I don't think anybody enjoys it more than I do. I enjoy it even if everything goes wrong. One bright afternoon several months ago I set out with four friends for an evening in Berkeley, where we had season tickets for the performances of the Berkeley Repertory Theatre. Sultana had prepared us a sumptuous picnic dinner with quiche, fresh bread and fruit, and two elaborate salads, which she packed carefully in the trunk. Halfway to Berkeley it started to rain.

We arrived at the university campus, hoping to find a warm, dry spot where we could eat, and discovered that the trunk of the car had suddenly decided that it was not going to open. We tried calling some locksmiths, but it seemed that was a busy night for locksmiths. So we tried several restaurants suitable for vegetarians, all of which were unfortunately closed. We made it to the theater just in time to see the curtain rise.

All the time this was happening, I was watching my mind. How would it react? I found it hadn't bothered me a bit that everything had gone wrong. We enjoyed ourselves anyway, simply being out together, and I felt as relaxed as if everything had gone precisely as planned. When your mind is still, you are free to enjoy whatever comes. This is a precious skill. My grandmother used to remind me often that ups and downs are the very texture of life. "But," she would add, "you don't have to go up and down with them."

Of course, I have to add that I have no objection to everything going smoothly. I don't look forward to fiascoes or complain, "Everything went just right. What a ghastly day!" I enjoy good news, a pleasant evening, a successful turn of events. Yet if you take my blood pressure on such occasions, you will find it completely normal: no excitement, just a quiet sense of joy. I have found that excitement, far from adding to enjoyment, actually takes away the capacity to enjoy.

After years of hammering away at them, I have been able to reduce my likes and dislikes to a negligible level. In most matters, I really do not have any personal preferences, which means that my mind almost never gets upset over any personal affront or inconvenience. All my vital energy is free to deal with the things in life that really matter: the welfare of others, the spiritual growth of those who look to me for guidance, problems like violence and stress-related disorders where the work of our meditation center can play a vital role.

It takes many years to realize the velocity of the thinking process, or the immense power behind its speed. The mind is a twelve-lane freeway, and mind-traffic obeys no known speed limits or driving laws. The whole purpose of meditation is to slow down the pace of this tumultuous traffic, and the struggle to do so can go on for years and years. Yet if you can bring the full power of your mind under control, you will have a turbocharged engine at your disposal. This is the only effective way to deal with stress and anxiety, and the only way to have true peace of mind. Then, instead of sticking to the old roads of conditioned living, you can have a real adventure: strike out cross-country into unexplored territory, where all your responses are free. You will be laying down a totally new road deep into consciousness, in search of a new land of love and joy.

[2]

Imagine if all things that are perishable grew still — for if we listen they are saying, "We did not make ourselves; he made us who abides forever" — imagine, then, that they should say this and fall silent, listening to the very voice of him who made them and not to that of his creation. . . .

In commenting on Augustine's second stanza, I want to try to bring to light some of the volcanic forces that work far, far below the surface strata of consciousness, forming the individual human personality as we see it — manifested in all the seemingly incomprehensible quirks of daily behavior. They are incomprehensible precisely because we are rarely able to see below the surface to what lies deep within: the currents which give rise to explosive emotional upheavals. All these wonders of the interior world we can see for ourselves when we take up the amazing journey into consciousness on the submarine that is meditation. This is a journey that takes us into the murky origins of our personal emotional responses to events around us. But we can travel deeper still: we can discover the place where the tremendous forces that ignite these responses can be resolved.

This is not at all a fantastical voyage. These descriptions do not proceed from the imagination of visionaries. When I point out landmarks along the way, they are landmarks which mystical pioneers like Francis and Augustine have discovered for themselves in the depths of their own consciousness. These landmarks exist; they are real. That is the reason why the journeys of the great mystics, as they themselves insist, are applicable to little people like you and me. In describing for us their routes in glowing words, they have furnished us with actual charts into deepest consciousness. By meditating profoundly, as they did, and following the same kind of challenging disciplines, you and I can discover these hidden territories for ourselves.

If we are to claim our rights to the enormous terrains within, with their untold wealth and precious human resources, there is no other way I know on earth than following for ourselves these same dynamic disciplines. Foremost among these, and indispensable, to my way of thinking, is the regular, systematic, and enthusiastic practice of meditation.

Let me begin by delving into the long development of the individual human personality. We can actually begin deep in the past, at a time when the earth itself was still being formed. We usually think of the earth as inert, inanimate. Let us for a moment think of it as Mother Earth, a living, loving woman. Bumper stickers remind us, "Every mother is a working mother." The earth too is a working mother, and she has to work hard indeed to support the array of plants and creatures — ourselves included — which make up her enormous brood. Just as remembering to love and respect our human mother for all she has done for us is a duty we should all hold dear, we should show the same kind of respect, consideration, and love for our mother the earth. This loving remembrance is the spiritual basis of ecology.

Corroboration for this animated view of the earth comes from a veteran science writer, Guy Murchie. "In a very real sense," Mr. Murchie writes, "the earth is alive like an animal. Like an animal it stirs in its sleep, it breathes air, it grows." In fact, the strange early picture of the earth that geophysicists have arrived at is reminiscent of the body of an adolescent, its muscles aching to exert themselves in the processes of expansion. "Its wounds heal; its juices circulate. Its skin metabolizes. Its nerves crackle quietly with vital messages." The story of the development of the human body, Murchie points out, is inextricably intertwined with that of the development of the earth. "My body was shaped in the rivers where vertebrates developed and lungs were born. And my apprenticeship was in the trees, where I grew my hands. . . . After the uplifting of the continents produced the grassy fields, I learned to stand up and look far, and outthink the lion."

In *Evolution and Ethics*, the eminent nineteenth-century biologist Thomas Huxley suggested another dimension to this picture of human evolution:

Every day experience familiarizes us with the facts which are grouped under the name of heredity. Every one of us bears upon him obvious marks of his parentage, perhaps of remoter relationships. More particularly, the sum of tendencies to act in a certain way, which we shall call "character," is often to be traced through a long series of progenitors and collaterals. So one may justly say that this "character" – this moral and intellectual essence of a man – does veritably pass out from one fleshly tabernacle to another, and does really transmigrate from generation to generation. In the newborn infant, the character lies latent, and is little more than a bundle of potentialities. But very early, these become actualities; they manifest themselves in dullness or brightness, weakness or strength, viciousness or uprightness; and with each feature modified by confluence with another's character, if by nothing else, the character passes on to its incarnation in new bodies. The Indian philosophers called character, as thus defined, "karma."

In five billion years the amoeba has become me. This is not a blind, arbitrary growth; each of us has played the major role in his or her own development. In every short lifetime, we are the result of what we have thought and done; at the end of each life, we shall be the sum total of all we have thought and done before.

Thinking, in this sense, can be construed as a rehearsal for action. This life of ours is full of the mind, actually made out of the mind: in Huxley's sense, a mind that can trace its continuity back over many previous generations. When Augustine began to see the extent of this process we call the mind, he was amazed:

> Great is this power of memory, exceedingly great, O my God, a spreading limitless room within me. Who can reach its uttermost depth? Here are men going afar to marvel at the heights of mountains, the mighty waves of the sea, the long courses of great rivers, the vastness of the ocean, the movements of the stars, yet they leave themselves unnoticed!
>
> In the innumerable fields and dens and caverns of my memory, innumerably full of innumerable kinds of things present either by their images or in themselves or by certain notions or moods . . . in and through all these does my mind range, and I move swiftly from one to another and penetrate them as deeply as I can, but find no end. So great is the force of memory, so great the force of life!

Some people, when faced with the force of our evolutionary past, throw up their hands and say, "I am powerless! My fate is already determined, and there is nothing I can do about it." They are ignoring the bright side to this mind of ours. There is no need to refer to any supernatural power, nor even to any external power, for escape; we shape our own destiny. My destiny has been placed entirely in my own hands. It is the continuous improvement I am able to make in the quality of my thinking that decides my rate of spiritual growth, decides the quality of my life today and of my life tomorrow. In a large measure, the quality of my thinking decides even my physical health – a fact that has some surprising implications.

As I said earlier, there is a quiet correspondence between the kind of body I have and the kind of mind I have. Each of us, by the thoughts we think and the actions we take, has influenced the physical body we inhabit and the physical environment in which that body moves. One Christian mystic exclaims, "My sin is stamped upon the universe!" Fortunately, the opposite is also true: each of us can say, "My goodness is stamped upon the universe." The fragment of divinity which is in me, which is in all creatures and all people of all races, has been revealed more and more, bit by bit, through this billion-year process of growth we call evolution, and it is continually being revealed anew. I can see this divine spark shining even through the eyes of our dogs. This awareness that they are not merely kith and kin, but living manifestations of the same spark of divinity, fills my heart with love for them. When this awareness dawns, it becomes a joyful responsibility to protect the lives of all creatures.

This divine spark travels through time from stage to stage of evolution. Our dog Ganesha reveals a little more of this spark than does, say, a tiger in the forest. Our main advance in evolution over the friendly animals is that we have the capacity to "look far," as Guy Murchie says, into the consequences of our actions.

Human beings who are violent of mind, in this view, still have one foot in the animal world. When we get angry, for instance, we do not think of the consequences of our words and actions, either for the victim of our anger or for ourselves. In this sense, no matter how much we may hail our times as the age of technological miracles, we are far from seeing the end of evolution.

In the history of the world there has been a certain blessed number of humans who have determined to go beyond their personal conditioning of mind and body so as to identify with the needs of all life. Such people, like Augustine or Teresa of Avila, may look like the rest of the human race to a casual observer, yet they no longer live in the limited, physical world. They live in the state we call God-consciousness, from which there is no fall. These pioneers in consciousness are able to show us a goal to which we should make every effort to direct our own individual evolution. By ourselves we would have a great deal of difficulty discerning this goal, for the increments by which we evolve toward it without intense personal effort are indeed small.

Looked at from a contemporary perspective – say, that of Einstein's "world line," the continuous thread that traces life through space and time – a fascinating picture emerges: of consciousness evolving through time, through the long travail of evolution, picking up conditioned responses in every individual creature's life and accumulating them in the collective heritage of humankind. To make the image even more picturesque, we can liken consciousness, traveling through time, to a wind: starting up as a tiny breeze, then picking up momentum as it adds responses, getting stronger and stronger as it blows through the phenomenal world to its end. Just as a wind blowing through a garden picks up a slight fragrance from the lilacs and roses and carries their fragrance on, though the lilac blossom and rose themselves may last only a couple of weeks, so the immaterial legacy of every life is carried by the wind of consciousness through evolution, and every creature is touched by it. Further – particularly in the human context – the conditioning and the responses of various creatures mingle and act on one another, so that this evolutionary heritage becomes richer and more complicated through time.

Of course, all this makes an extremely elaborate picture. In a sense, we can look on one person's anger as a million years old! That is why retaliation makes absolutely no sense: patience, given the whole history of human personality, is much the most sensible policy. Besides anger, fortunately, we have some redeeming qualities mixed in too: a bit of tenderness, an underlying willingness to forgive. As Augustine observed:

> Who can map out the various forces at play in one soul? Man is a great depth, O Lord. The hairs of his head are easier by far to count than his feelings, the movements of his heart.

Of all these negative forces and feelings, I would call anger the single emotion most characteristic of our times, so much so that this could be called the Age of Rage. Angry, violent personalities are offered in contemporary entertainment and taken as models of behavior. Even the news media, for some reason, seem to consider it a duty to bring violent heroes and heroines before our eyes – if possible, every day. All this adds immeasurably to the burden of violent conditioning which each of us carries through this lifetime.

This seemingly imaginative history has very practical contributions to make to our understanding of personal problems. When a person comes into this life with certain pronounced proclivities, such as a tendency to erupt in rage, he is going to find himself again and again in frustrating situations where the pent-up hostilities inside him ferment until they find violent outlets. In this view, such people are as much the cause of these situations as they are victims of circumstance. They cannot avoid responsibility for getting into frustrating situations, any more than they can avoid responsibility for their anger.

As a result, if this proclivity goes unchecked, they may well develop serious health problems. Some researchers, for example, have drawn a connection between an anger-prone personality and heart disease. I find this quite reasonable, for anger places the heart and the rest of the circulatory system under tremendous stress. Digestive problems may well be another long-term correlate: a person prone to anger may develop an ulcer in the digestive tract because the stomach will be in turmoil much of the time. Of course, I am not denying that external factors play a part in bringing on ill health. Yet the mystics go far deeper: they point out that we actually bring with us into this life the tendencies that lead us into the activities, occupations, relationships, and behavior which bring these external factors onto the scene. When they say that we are responsible even for our health, they are not being occult; they are talking good, sound sense.

Yet, as I said, there is a very hopeful side of this comprehensive picture of evolution. No matter what our tendencies, each one of us has a choice. Even if we come from an angry home, went to school with angry teachers and classmates, and have an angry partner, spiritual disciplines can help us to use the same context and relationships to improve the quality of our life. This is the glory of the human being: we always have that choice. So when you are living with angry people, put up with them cheerfully and don't withdraw your support from them. It will help them a good deal, but even more, it will help you. It will not only undo some of the angry conditioning which you brought with you into this life, but also add greatly to your stock of patience, good will, and compassion. All this is the best health insurance I know.

This is going to be tough. Yet if I may be a bit morbid in the interests of highlighting choices, isn't surgery tough? Surgery is a frightful procedure, as any sensitive physician will admit. I can appreciate a man like Norman Cousins saying that to go into the intensive care unit of a hospital will upset any normal human being. Surely, artificial valves and the like are helpful. Yet these and similar remedies are meant only to deal with symptoms; the real cause of our physical problems – for instance, anger – usually goes untouched. How can the symptoms not reappear in time?

Former Secretary of State Dean Rusk once remarked that partial disarmament is like building a bridge halfway across a river. From the spiritual view of health, surgery and pharmacology are the same: they are partial solutions, a bridge halfway across the chasm of ill health. I do understand that there are special circumstances which call for surgery. But even then, to achieve real, lasting health we have to change our way of thinking: not merely our lifestyle but our thought-style. This is where meditation comes in.

Some of the most magnificent figures in the history of mysticism have begun with severe emotional problems, even serious physical handicaps. So there is no need for any of us to feel downcast about our situation or the particular difficulties we face, provided we do everything we can to purify our mind. Meditation is essentially a discipline for slowing down the furious activity of the mind; and if you can gradually bring your mind to a state so still that no movement, no thought, can arise except those you yourself approve, your mind will have become pure. We have no need to teach pure motives to the mind. All that is necessary to make the mind pure is to undo the negative conditioning to which it has been subjected; then we will be left with pure, unconditioned awareness. "Be still," the Bible says, "and know that I am God."

We can call this long process character rebuilding. Our first character in this life has been inherited: prefabricated, if you like, for the most part by negative conditioning. In this, I am grieved to admit, most of us have precious little say. Now it is our job to rebuild our character, almost from the foundation up. The priceless advice of the mystics is that inside, at the core of our being, we already have a Resident Architect, and that our first task – in which they are more than willing to help us – is to come up with an appropriate set of blueprints.

When we meditate on passages which bear the imprint of these pure minds' experiences of God, we find that their words are like the working drawings a contractor follows. "Let the scriptures be the countenance of God," Augustine advises. "Look into the scriptures, the eyes of your heart on its heart." This is exactly what we are doing in meditation when we give all our concentration to the words of an inspirational passage like this one from Augustine: we sink gradually into the heart of the author's experience until we see through his or her eyes. At the end of this book I give a list of such passages from scripture and the mystical giants of the Christian tradition. They make perfect blueprints for this job of character rebuilding.

⟿

I touched earlier on the subject of anxiety. With crippling emotional ailments so common today, this is a terribly important subject. Here I would like to venture a few suggestions about the nature of anxiety, which will make clear how closely it ties in with the picture of personality development I have just described.

Wisps of anxiety float into the lives of even very successful people. They can afflict even those who are blessed with abundant health. There is no easy way to account for these wisps, and most of us can find no safe bastion against them. Yet isn't it telling that in a civilization where dependence on external satisfactions is most marked, anxiety is epidemic?

Imagine if the ball-and-socket joint in your hip were dislocated. Your leg would be out of joint, and you would not be able to do much of anything without being aware of the discomfort twenty-four hours a day. You could not sit anywhere without thinking about it. The slightest movement would make you wince, and walking would become an excruciating chore. The mind can get out of joint like this too, so that we go through life with everything a little off, a little wrong. Many people today report a strange sense of not being at home anywhere, of not fitting in; often they use words like "loneliness" or "alienation." Whatever they try to do, part of them seems to wish they were doing something else instead. Frustration at not being able to curb these symptoms can lead to severe depression. Often the perpetrator of this kind of trouble is anxiety, and it needs to be interpreted from a depth which secular psychology cannot reach.

Anxiety can be particularly acute when we find ourselves confronted by death. This gives another valuable clue to its origin. Most of us find the death of another person or creature deeply unsettling, yet after a time we usually manage to submerge our feelings and carry on. For someone deeply sensitive to the transitory nature of life, however, an encounter with death can leave scars that last a lifetime. As a teenager Augustine witnessed the untimely death of a bosom friend, and suddenly a trapdoor opened into deeper awareness. He was devastated. "I thought death suddenly capable of devouring all men, because he had taken this loved one."

In the very depths of our consciousness, which we can call the collective unconscious, is written the story of our evolution in its entirety. Millions of times during the course of our evolution we have suffered the loss of our parents, our partners, our children, our friends. Millions of times we ourselves have gone through the agonies of death. In the unconscious is a complete record of all this – not so much of the details, but certainly of the main events. Just as each of us bears the physical marks of millions of years of evolution, mentally too we have a complete library of subtle impressions gleaned from the last five billion years: instincts, primal emotions, the deeply conditioned responses of fight and flight, and much, much more.

The main reason why none of us are consciously aware of these deep, traumatic records is that life would then be impossible for us. Who would be able to sleep in peace tonight if he remembered all the times that parents and children, partner and partner, friend and friend have been parted? I am not speaking here about a mere intellectual awareness that all of us are born to die. If you knew in your heart that everybody is bound to be parted by death, you would find it terribly difficult to carry on the routine of everyday life. For this crucial reason the mind has drawn a merciful veil over the contents of the unconscious, allowing human beings to go on living "in the valley of the shadow of death."

The word "anxiety" is an exceptionally weak term for expressing the depths of feeling from which arises this vague uneasiness, this unsettled sense of being out of place and running out of time. Generally we can only ascribe it to external events, if we succeed in linking it to anything at all. But what is actually happening is that a wisp of memory is rising, whispering to us from deep within that nothing external in life is secure, nothing physical ever lasts. The body wears out; the senses grow dull and the intellect feeble; no relationship between two physical creatures, no matter how loving, outlasts the passage of time. These are the sorry facts of life. The astonishing thing is that even though we study biology and see old age and death coming to people on every side, in our heart of hearts none of us believe that this is going to happen to us too. Even so, through all the discreet veils that are cast over the immense canyons of the unconscious, faint wisps like mist rising out of mountain valleys escape through tiny crevices in the mind and come floating up into daily life. Such are the deep springs of anxiety.

No matter how hard we may try, in the long run none of us can escape the devastating fact of death. Yet an encounter with death, as in the case of Augustine, can leave us changed decidedly for the better. It can prompt us forward on the long search for something secure in life, something that death cannot reach.

Many people, of course, do not particularly desire to be prompted forward like this. "I don't like to think about such things," they may say. "I'm happier carrying on as if nothing is going to happen." For such people, the mystics have a penetrating question: If you are truly happy inside, why do you feel the need to go looking for happiness outside? This is spiritual logic at its deadliest. It is because we need some temporary relief from these nagging, floating wisps that we go around shopping for pleasures. Though we may not admit it willingly, those who have experimented to a reasonable extent with the smorgasbord of physical

feelings. "I get hurt very easily," we say, "so please be extra nice to me." It is really an implied threat. Isn't there a shrub called "sensitive plant," which you have only to touch lightly for all the leaves to droop and hide? This is what most of us mean by being sensitive: ignore us for a little while or chance to say the wrong thing, and emotionally we fold right up. I would not call this sensitivity; it is simply preoccupation with oneself. The only kind of sensitivity worth cultivating is sensitivity to the needs of others, and to cultivate that, preoccupation with ourselves has to be reduced.

Most people cannot be very compassionate towards others for the simple reason that they are not sensitive to anyone except themselves. The less you dwell on yourself, the more your sensitivity will open out to the needs and feelings of others. Every time you hurt someone and then grieve inside because of it, you are attending a valuable seminar on sensitivity. It is a seminar on the deepest and most personal level, the experiential, and it is infinitely more effective than anything we can attend for college credit. The credit comes to us directly, when we change our behavior and don't hurt people again. "Everybody's feelings can be hurt," we realize, "just like my own. I have to take others' feelings into consideration in everything I do."

In learning how to make good use of pain, we can gain helpful clues from men who know pain well: boxers. When you have a strong desire to strike out at someone – probably it is someone with whom you are emotionally involved – part of your mind is convinced that yielding to this urge will bring you satisfaction. That is the basic problem. If you have some measure of detachment at the crucial moment, you can actually watch the urge get hold of your right hand and drag you into the ring to take a swing. At that time, if you can be sensitive to the pain you will cause the other person, you can free your hand from the urge's grip.

Gradually, after a great struggle, you can build up the strength of will to deliver a left hook to the bullying urge itself. The person who is going to feel the force of the blow, of course, is you: the part of you that is entangled in wanting to strike out. That is the painful part of it all. But in the long run, it is also you who will be free.

I have seen snapshots in the newspaper of chaps after a rugged bout: battered beyond belief. Yet their desire to win was so great that they were hardly aware of the pain. They were so concentrated on the glory and the adulation and the cash that goes with winning that a lot of the capacity to feel pain was flowing into that. Similarly, we can actually come to feel a fierce sense of joy in battling these entrenched urges that have dominated our lives, and in seeing them hit the canvas – finally, for good.

These are all clues to the mind's real capacities for self-help. That is why I say that the way to deal with mental anguish is to dig deeper and discover a more profound source of motivation. Your energy will flow into that, just as water flows to a lower level. That is exactly how desire flows to deeper sources of satisfaction than the ones which promise purely personal gain.

Look back on some of the moments in your life when you were longing for something very much. Weren't you able to endure pain cheerfully at such times for the sake of the greater joy to come? Similarly, all of us find joy in suffering a personal loss for the sake of someone we love. We can learn to feel such love for more and more people; it is at bottom a matter of extending our sensitivity. This can go to such an extent that if somebody is pointedly unkind to us, our immediate response will be to feel sorry for that person. No urge to strike back will be able to get a grip on our mind. Even when we have to oppose a person we can work this miracle, which is what is meant by "fighting the sin but winning over the sinner." Then the mystics ask a marvelous question: when you find joy in suffering so that others can benefit, how can sorrow come to you?

The best way of dealing with anxiety and distress, therefore, is not to run away from them but to see them as tugging at our sleeves, trying to be helpful. "Go ahead," they are trying to tell us, "take a look inside!" That is precisely what meditation is: a conscious, controlled look inside. When anxiety is so deep-rooted, after all, it is not to be dispelled. It has something to teach us. Once, in the middle of an impassioned sermon, Augustine stopped, looked at his parishioners a few moments, and said musingly:

"You are thinking that I am saying what I always say; and you go on doing what you always do." Then a fiery sobriety came into his voice: "Change, change, I beseech you! The end of life is always unpredictable. Each man walks with a chance of falling." In order to effect real changes in our life, changes that can leave us vastly better able to deal with the exigencies of human existence, it is essential to learn to control in some measure this unpredictable thinking process of ours.

↜

The first way in which meditating regularly can be of immediate help is in teaching us to increase our powers of concentration. In every possible arena of life, learning to improve concentration is as important as striving to lessen likes and dislikes, which I have already discussed at length. By now I need only a couple of minutes' observation to gauge a person's powers of concentration and to guess with fair accuracy at the problems he or she may be having in daily living. Poor concentration brings problems everywhere.

Most of us have much better concentration than we imagine. When you are doing something you enjoy immensely, don't you find you can give it your attention easily? That is the marvel of concentration, and joy flows from it naturally. All of us possess this capacity in some measure. To deepen it and bring it under our beck and call, we need to work on extending it to illumine activities and people which at present we do not particularly enjoy. This too, you can see, comes down to overcoming likes and dislikes, which are a constant source of trouble in daily life.

The gains will be notable on many fronts. For one, thoughts from the past cannot break in on the person who has developed his concentration. He has built a kind of citadel around his mind, a great fortress in the tradition of the most memorable ever to be constructed on medieval European mountaintops. Images and impressions from the past, fears and dreams of the future, cannot enter that fortress unbidden. Attention is a drawbridge that he can lower whenever he chooses.

On the other hand, those of us who have not developed our powers of concentration in this way are as vulnerable as cities with low walls. Any anxiety, any fear, any petty desire can jump over the walls and disrupt the mind whenever it likes. This is one reason I find it so easy to sympathize with the plight of our young people today: they have precious little opportunity to develop their concentration. Their attention span seems to be broken up into smaller and smaller fragments of time: in school, in their recreation, and particularly by the media. It frightens me to see some of the difficulties they are headed for in life.

To bring all this down to a mundane level, I could easily write a book on the spiritual side of shopping. Here you are, wanting to pick up a new umbrella, and you step into a department store. There are a lot of things to see in such a store, all cunningly arranged so that in order to get at anything, you have to look at everything else first. An hour or two later you emerge with bagfuls of articles, none of which you needed when you went in. I have seen this happen hundreds of times. In such cases, the mind is not content with waiting for distractions to jump over its walls and get in; it is so eager to be distracted that it jumps over its own walls and runs about the store like a willful child.

In shopping, I would say, make up your mind in advance exactly what you want to buy; then go in, pick up what is on your list without looking left or right, and rush straight for the exit, preferably stopping at the cashier's on your way. Only upon reaching the safety of the sidewalk should you pause to catch your breath. These days this is largely a question of self-defense. Surviving a shopping trip calls for concentration and detachment, a valuable commodity which most retailers assume their customers lack completely.

Another benefit, less prosaic, is this: when you have trained your mind to concentrate, it cannot get trapped in an old memory. To get trapped, the mind has to leave the freeway of attention at an off-ramp. Usually what happens is that instead of heading directly for San Francisco, say, you look around suddenly, see the Bay directly in front, and realize with a jolt that you have taken the wrong exit and are heading for the Richmond Bridge. "Well, I've come this far," you sigh. "I might as well just go to Berkeley instead." This is the way most of us go through a normal day, never quite sure where we are going to end up. Then, at the end of each distracting thought, we are faced with the problem of how to get back on the road where we last turned off. If we can learn to keep our attention in one lane most of the time, which is what sustained concentration amounts to, we will actually find it difficult to get trapped in memories of any kind. We will be amazed at how much anxiety, much of which is triggered by ancient memories, will then disappear from our life.

The applications of improved concentration go much deeper than we may think. Even in the most intimate of personal relationships, most of us still live inside our own private mental worlds. The walls between us and the realms of the past are so low that our attention is often occupied in the past instead of the present, leaving us very little attention to give to those we want to love. Despite our best intentions to draw closer, all kinds of distracting thoughts – likes and dislikes, attachments and aversions, private moods, dreams and desires – come in anytime they like, keeping other people at a distance. We yearn for closeness and find, more often, disappointment.

Here Augustine echoes the experiences that almost all of us go through, starting often in our adolescence. "What I needed most was to love and to be loved. I rushed headlong into love, eager to be caught. Happily I wrapped those painful bonds around me; and sure enough, I would be lashed with the red-hot pokers of jealousy, by suspicions and fear, by bursts of anger and quarrels." The journey into deeper consciousness is one we must take up if ever we are to find the love, the closeness, and the fulfillment we all so earnestly desire.

[3]

> . . . so that we should hear not his word through the tongues of men, nor the voice of angels, nor the clouds' thunder, nor any symbol, but the very Self which in these things we love, and strain beyond ourselves to attain a flash of that eternal wisdom which abides above all things. . . .

In talking about deeper levels of consciousness, I realize I am asking for a leap of the imagination. Let me try to make these levels more real by giving you a concrete metaphor.

Imagine swimming around in a very deep lake: the lake of the mind. We know how to swim effortlessly on the surface; modern life is quite good at teaching us all kinds of ingenious strokes for this. It supplies us with Styrofoam lounge chairs to keep us floating pleasurably on the surface of life forever. Yet the sensitive person, whatever his or her station, cannot help becoming aware over time how much distress is involved in the struggle merely to stay afloat. For some reason, peace of mind simply doesn't seem attainable; the mind seems to be capable of stirring up a never-ending succession of waves.

Life on the shimmering surface of consciousness,

we are someday forced to admit, isn't everything it's supposed to be. We come to the uncomfortable realization that there is simply no guarantee of security anywhere in life on the surface, no thing or situation to hold on to. At some point, sooner or later, every sensitive person reaches a certain level of frustration where he or she is ready to dive, if only to find out what lies below.

Yet this doesn't mean that doubts don't remain. Turning inwards can be a frightening prospect. Most people feel nervous when they don't have anything to look at; their attention is used to homesteading in their eyes. They have to have some noise to listen to, or they become uneasy; their ears cannot deal with the void. That is human conditioning. Sooner or later, most of us encounter the haunting fear that if we turn our senses inwards, which is what diving into the murky waters of consciousness means, we may lose everything enjoyable in life. This fear is one of the most formidable obstacles between us and the capacity to dive deeper.

Most of us accept this barrier. "Oh, that's how my desires are," we say. "They flow in every direction, and there's nothing I can do about it." I say, "You can do a great deal about it." We can learn to deepen some desire-channels and fill up others. When our desire flows compulsively toward overeating, for example, that is a simple matter of never having tried hard enough to curtail the flow of desire when it was smaller. Every kind of addiction begins like this. Then, once the channel has been cut, attention flows into it without even asking our permission; that is what conditioning means. It is for this reason that I speak so often about the need to train our senses: vigilance keeps habits and addictions from taking undue advantage of us, from turning us into victims. Yet even if we have allowed ourselves to be victimized, any conditioned habit can be changed through the practice of meditation; even the strongest addiction can be undone.

The practical element in training the senses is willpower. I used to have many friends who counted themselves beatniks, and their frankness could be quite disarming; when I talked about the importance of willpower, they would sigh and say, "We don't have any!" Even if you find yourself in this embarrassing situation, you can build up a strong will with two simple exercises. One is to train your senses vigilantly; the other, which I will take up in a minute, is to work on letting go of selfish attachments. Both can be painful, but both are extremely rewarding as well.

Meditation is the king of interior engineering projects. Through it we can divert the flow of our attention from channels of desire we do not approve and direct it into new channels of thinking, feeling, and responding. "If a man will work an inward work," Meister Eckhart says beautifully of this kind of engineering, "he must pour all his powers into himself as into a corner of the soul, and must hide himself from all images and forms. Then he can work." That describes meditation very well. What it can do is truly amazing, as you can discover for yourself. I have seen long-standing addictions simply fall away from people who are meditating sincerely. Meditation cut a new channel for the vital energy which flowed toward that particular desire; as that energy began to flow elsewhere, the addiction lost its power to command attention and withered away, much like a plant that ceases to receive water. Instead of watering a compulsive habit like overeating, vital energy began to flow toward goals that are much more deeply fulfilling.

When you can sink to deeper and deeper levels of consciousness in meditation, you will find that attention flows naturally back to its source like creeks of vital energy – from the eyes, from the ears, from all the senses. On the surface, if it seems to you that you don't have much energy or willpower, the reason may be that a good deal of energy is flowing into these sense-creeks without your even being aware of it. In meditation, instead of flowing outward, this vitality begins to be consolidated as a huge reservoir of energy within.

⇴

The second great obstacle to diving into deeper consciousness is the fear of giving up strong personal attachments. For most of us, our strongest attachments are to people. But I am not saying we should give up close, loving relationships. The precious secret we can learn here is that when we give up our selfish attachments to people, we can draw closer to them than ever before.

Most of us assume that by wrapping our attachments tighter and tighter around us, like a life jacket, we can manage to stay afloat in the storms of life. This belief is one of the basic currents in our conditioning, dating perhaps from a very early age of evolution when survival was the day-to-day challenge of existence. But fierce personal attachment has long since outlived its place in the human scheme of things. Augustine describes our predicament vividly:

> I was held back by mere trifles, the most paltry inanities, all my old attachments. They plucked at my garments of flesh and whispered: "Are you going to dismiss us? From this moment we shall never be with you again, for ever and ever. From this moment you will never again be allowed to do this thing, or that, for evermore"– things so sordid that I beg you in your mercy to keep the soul of your servant free from them.

In reality, selfish attachments only keep us from seeing beneath the separate surface of life, where constant change and turmoil are the law. Instead of a life jacket, they turn out to be a straitjacket.

Personal entanglements are like the lotus plants with rose and white petals that used to flourish in the ponds around the village where I grew up. After a strenuous game of soccer under the hot tropical sun, we boys loved to go swimming in those ponds, and one of the games we liked best was a kind of underwater tag. If you know about lotuses, you know that hundreds of tentacle-like vines rise up through the water from the mud deep below to support the delicate flowers you see floating so calmly on the surface. Just when you are trying to dive quickly to avoid being tagged by your pursuer, those vines can wrap themselves around you. The more you flail and try to pry yourself loose, the more you get entangled. Many times I have seen a friend have to be rescued from their clutches before he ran out of breath and drowned in their embrace.

Where I see passionate entanglements played up mercilessly today is in the exploitation of "sex appeal." Everybody, for every apparent purpose from art to advertising, seems to be trying to get in on the act. To take one ridiculous instance, why I should be lured to buy a particular model of car because it has sex appeal has always been a mystery to me. There is no earthly connection. This unceasing emphasis on the physical element of life is doing untold damage to relations between man and woman. In any relationship based on physical attraction, heartbreak has to follow. In a play I saw recently one character observes trenchantly that the average lifetime of such a relationship is ten days!

Each of us has been through relationships like this. The question is not so much whether physical attraction is an appropriate basis for a relationship; I would say it is no basis whatsoever. Physical attraction is never constant. It sets in motion a cycle of expectation and disillusionment that can go on and on and on. Often we have to learn to live with a high level of anxiety in such relationships, which over time destroys our emotional security, disturbs our peace of mind, and can even wreck our health. Some relationships never recover from the effects.

In something so basic, so strongly conditioned, as physical attraction, any amount of advice has practical limitations. We may have to go through such a relationship more than once to see for ourselves how most of the rewards we fantasize about go to pieces. The person who lives in a world of fantasy will often blame the other for letting him down. Perhaps, for example, Juliet expects Romeo to come to her balcony every morning and launch into "It is the east, and you are the sun . . ." Three days after the honeymoon, she feels crushed when she is greeted at breakfast with nothing more romantic than "Where's the coffee?" Many torrid relationships sputter because of just such inflated expectations, which demand of life something that it simply cannot give.

Yet I am not trying to imply that close relationships are impossible. Through experience, most of us come to realize that in love nothing comes as easily as we expected. Everything beautiful has to be worked for. We need to begin by accepting each other as we are, but we also need to help each other to grow. Both partners should support each other tenderly while working to overcome their drawbacks, trying always to put each other first so that they enlarge the area where the circles of their lives overlap. Finally the great day will come when those circles are not two but one. Then every day will be full of joy.

The desire to draw closer to others is our inherent wealth in life; to try to deny it is dangerous in the extreme. Instead of being driven by it or trying to suppress it, we can learn to harness this tremendous drive so that its enormous power and wealth of feeling flow into our daily life. Then our love will reach out to everybody, and all who come within our orbit will feel its healing effects. This is capitalizing on the propensity that every one of us has to get attached, instead of letting it lead us around by the nose.

The surest way to do this is easy to understand. All of us have a deep desire to love and to be loved; we can learn to expand that desire to wanting everybody around us to be loved. Instead of considering only our own needs, we can begin by thinking more about the needs of our immediate family. Wherever we go, wherever we are, we can remind ourselves to remember the needs of those around us and ask if we are helping to meet those needs. The result will be a tremendous consolidation of vitality; for there will be that much less time and attention for worry, anxiety, diffidence, or depression.

When we are kind and helpful to people around us – when we are tender to our neighbors' children, for instance, just as if they were our own – we are really harnessing this great drive for affection. Ultimately it can reach the size of a well-managed river, bringing love to everybody. That is the power of attachment, and that is the wider purpose for which it was certainly created. Everybody has this power in abundance, and everybody has trouble harnessing it too. Don't despair, therefore, if it takes a lot of work to remove the selfish element from your relationships. The more people you can love, the freer you will be in every situation, and the less you will be troubled by the urge to get emotionally entangled with one or two. Even your most intimate relationships will flourish as a result.

Here again meditation comes in. The words of the inspirational passage can open an arrow's entry into deeper consciousness, especially in times of tribulation. Through that tiny opening you can peer straight down into the recesses of the mind, thousands of fathoms deep, where our desires are unified, everybody's best interests are the same, and the qualities of compassion and forgiveness reign. If you can keep your attention focused on that shaft of light, help can come to you from the very depths of consciousness, from your own deepest resources of divinity. Augustine describes such an experience:

> That was all, just not to desire what I wanted and to want what you wished. But where was my free will in that grueling time? From what deep recess was it called up at that turning point, in which I bent my neck to your light yoke?

The darker side of selfish attachments is a grueling lesson to learn. Gradually, however, with experience, our faith grows that deep within us the Lord is willing and able to take responsibility for our ultimate welfare. Slowly we can surrender our personal will to his immeasurably more profound purpose. Bit by bit, we can work ourselves loose from the grip of compulsive emotional entanglements in the faith that our capacity to love and be loved will thereby be magnified a millionfold.

꘎

Just as every country has its own geographic and cultural milieu, every region of the mind, every level of consciousness, has certain salient characteristics. Traveling to these inner continents is very much like visiting foreign lands. As we move into these subconscious realms, one of the first startling landmarks comes when the senses suddenly take their bags and say, "This is where we get off." They grab their guitars and tennis racquets, pick up their bulging suitcases, and wave: "See you when you get back!" From that point on, we will find that our concentration improves dramatically.

When I first descended into these fascinating depths in the early days of my meditation, I observed that as long as I did not attempt to follow any association of thoughts, my concentration was generally very good. But as soon as I followed even a legitimate line of thinking, such as reasoning about the meaning of the words, my mind would slip surreptitiously off the freeway of concentration and onto a detour. For someone whose concentration had always been an asset, this was a revealing surprise. Since then I have come to the sad conclusion that half the trouble the mind gets us into is the result not so much of thinking but of thinking about thinking. There is literally no end to it. To avoid this kind of exhausting mental meandering, we need to learn how to dive to a level of consciousness so deep that thoughts themselves are suspended, where the thinking process is stilled.

If we work at spiritual disciplines diligently, there comes a time when we find ourselves standing in a land where thought has no visa, not even as a tourist. The customs officer on the dock points his finger ceremoniously and says, "Sorry, but you thoughts won't be needed here." On their way back up the gangway to the ship, thoughts meet words coming down with all their baggage. "We were sent back," they say. "How can you guys expect to be allowed in?" It is this land, where the mind is utterly still, that Augustine is trying to give us a glimpse of in this passage I have called "Entering into Joy."

In the beginning, it is a rather disorienting place. We are used to navigating with the mind and senses; when they are temporarily left behind, we need time to get our bearings and learn to walk. Augustine describes this as "a lamentable darkness in which my latent possibilities are hidden from myself, so that my mind, questioning itself upon its own powers, feels that it cannot rightly trust its own report." This kind of experience marks the beginning of true detachment from the mind.

I can illustrate with a more familiar situation. When I go into a movie theater for a bargain matinee, for a few moments I can't see a thing. My eyes, used to the dazzling California sunlight outside, are temporarily rendered useless, and I have no idea of where to find a seat. This is somewhat the way it feels to plunge below the level of discursive thought in meditation: you don't see anything that looks like life as we know it, and you feel blind and confused. You are entering the unconscious, trying to become conscious, and everything is unfamiliar.

In this sense, teachers like Augustine function somewhat like movie ushers who come up to us in the darkness and say, "Do you see that corner there? Fourth row to the left; there's a seat right by the aisle." We stand still for a few minutes, and soon we can make out a few heads directly in front. Finally we can see the seats and reach them without stumbling. The same thing happens in meditation; it is simply a matter of training our inward eyes.

Don't children attending their first swimming lessons have a healthy fear of putting their faces under water? They are afraid they are going to drown. This is the feeling we can get when we begin to break loose from some of our long-cherished emotional attachments. When I was first meditating, I had the same fears all of you must have. All kinds of struggles were going on inside me, and it took time and effort to overcome them. But once the waters closed over my head and I began to get my bearings in these new realms, I knew this was what I had been looking for and longing for, and all my energy went into diving deeper.

Experience has taught me that when we put our heads under and dive deep, leaving selfish attachments on the surface, we find a joy that is a million times what any surface sensation can give, and a love that at its fullest expression embraces all of life. Every mystic gives us this same assurance: you feel like a fish swimming in the sea of light, of love, of joy that is the Lord. When you face the fear of losing these sensory satisfactions, try to remember that what is waiting for you far below the surface is infinite joy, infinite love, infinite life.

Remember this too when you find yourself getting wrapped up in the events of the day. Whatever you are enmeshed in personally during the day, part of your attention in meditation will be on that. It will act like an inflatable inner tube around your middle, preventing you from diving below the surface. No attachment is worth the price you will be paying: you can take my word for it, and the word of the world's great saints and mystics too. I assure you that in letting go of personal attachments, you are not losing anything except your frustration; you are not letting go of anything but your old insecurities.

While you are meditating, don't be thinking about

anything whatsoever. Concentrate completely on the inspirational passage. When your concentration is complete, you will not have any impediments on the surface; you will sink naturally deeper and deeper. Then no distraction will have any compelling force behind it. It will not bother you; it will not oppress you; it will have no power to deflect you from your purpose. Eventually you will reach a level where selfish desires won't even come to you any more; only the desires you desire will come to you. In no way do you lose your capacity to desire. What you gain is freedom.

⌯

Augustine's expression "strain beyond ourselves," in my practical interpretation, implies that we must push the frontiers of our awareness deeper and deeper.

When we are able to travel into the deepest recesses of consciousness, we discover that we need no longer be hemmed in by circumstances or personality traits or even by the conditioning of our past. In a sense, each of us is a child of our past. Our childhood upbringing, our neighborhood environment and the cultural milieu in which we grew up, the schools we attended, the movies we have seen, the books and magazines and newspapers we have read, the company we have kept – all these have molded our present character and conduct. Yet when we travel deeper into consciousness and approach the forbid-

in expressing their frustration and put that energy to use undoing the damage that has been done.

As we travel deeper into consciousness, we find we can push many of our limitations further and further. We can give ourselves room to move about in, room to expand. We need no longer live with the vague feeling of being crimped, cabined, and confined.

The vast majority of people, to take just one illustration, keep very little distance between the way their minds work and the way they themselves act. This is a very restrictive habit. When I was on the faculty of my university in India, we used to see Hollywood films in which a ventriloquist named Edgar Bergen appeared with a puppet called Charlie McCarthy. Mr. Bergen would place Charlie on his knee and ask solicitously, "What do you want?" Charlie would say, "A good, stiff drink." Most of our urges, I think, have learned over time to be ventriloquists much more accomplished than Edgar Bergen. We come home from the office tired and tense and our body announces, "I need a good, stiff drink!" We don't stop to realize that this is merely the mind doing its routine. Mental urges, in fact, are past masters of this devious art. Like everyone else, I too used to be under the mistaken impression that my mind and I were one and the same; when my mind urged me in a polished, well-inflected voice to do something, I actually used to go out and act on it. Today, after years of training myself not to identify with the mind, I sometimes get amused remembering this. "Here you are, a reasonably bright fellow, able to lecture at length on English literature and the mechanics of language. How could you possibly have fallen for this ego ventriloquist?" As my meditation deepened, I learned how to keep more distance from these promptings. If my mind began to complain about someone, I wouldn't allow it to influence my words or actions. I was free to choose my own responses: kind words, patience, and respect.

Most emotional problems, I have since found, can be solved with this one master strategy: put some distance between yourself and your mind. It calls for a lot of daring, I admit. But in this country you have been brought up in a society that sets a premium on daring; why not put it to the best use possible? You will not only be getting over your resentment of a particular person; you will also be getting over the tendency to waste time and precious energy resenting. When you gain this kind of detachment from the mind, life loses most of its sorrow and frustration. You can listen to opposition with complete respect, without ever compromising your own views.

I have attended a great many committee meetings in my lifetime; on a large university campus like the one where I taught, difficult issues have to be discussed frequently, and on each issue different people can hold very different points of view. But the biggest obstacle to easy communication and the resolution of important issues, I found, was not differences of opinion; it was lack of respect for other people. In my experience, the person who doesn't respect other opinions is the person who is inclined to believe that he knows everything and nobody else knows anything. Others are not likely to support him in this position, so he generally finds himself in a distinct minority. Working to respect the opinions of others is an effective way to encourage detachment in ourselves, and it brings a good deal of peace of mind as well.

Whatever your mind is saying, try to listen to it with detachment. If it insists, "This is what you want," you should furrow your brow and counter, "How do you know?" This can save you so many health problems, so many emotional crises, so much frustration and unnecessary heartbreak. It will be a struggle, but you have my assurance, and the assurance of great mystics like Augustine, that it is a struggle you cannot lose. This doesn't mean that your life will be free from quarrels or that you will never again find yourself in tense situations; these are the texture of life. But if you can gain this kind of detachment, the agitation in your mind will be kept to a minimum, the wear and tear on your nervous system will be much less, and you will be free from that sinking feeling that you haven't done very well in your relationships.

⟜

More than on any other quality, I believe, winning lasting freedom depends on the cultivation of plain, simple patience. It is impatient people who are liable to get suddenly anxious or discourteous. Patience acts as a shield against inner turmoil of every kind. It keeps the mind steady even in the midst of turbulent situations, which is one of the secrets of maintaining robust health. Patience is true preventive medicine on every front.

We can develop patience quite simply by pushing in the direction of patience: greater and greater patience, more and more often, in the everyday vicissitudes of life's normal situations and relationships. When you try to be more patient with someone difficult, you are extending the limits of your patience. When you refuse to act on anger or frustration even when provoked, you are deepening your own security. Every day you can go to bed knowing that your limitations have been pushed back a little more, that a little more negative conditioning has been erased.

Gradually we are working our way toward a critical realization: we can actually go beyond the mechanisms of the mind entirely. Thinking, however useful it may be at times, is not the highest human faculty; it is only a stage in development. If, for example, in the throes of evolution we had stopped with instinct, saying, "This is the highest possible mode of knowing," our human future would have been stunted: I would not be seated here writing these words, nor would you be reading them. Like instinct, reason is only a way station. When friends and I go to Berkeley to see a play, we sometimes stop halfway along to stretch our legs. But we don't get so involved in stretching legs that we forget to go on to the theater. Thought, in the same vein, is a useful but temporary stopping station; it should not be considered a permanent solution to the problems of living. Just as we were able to rise above instinct and to develop reason, if not always common sense, the mystics say we should learn to pass at will beyond discursive thinking and enter into a higher mode of knowing.

The way people sometimes praise the achievements of this century, you would think they have concluded that this is journey's end; we have made it. I think we are entitled to question whether we have even arrived at an age of reason, much less of higher awareness. When the age of reason is established, the nations of the world will not spend a million dollars a minute on destroying each other. Nobody will feel compelled to advertise harmful habits in prestigious magazines. We will make only things that are useful and beneficial, and we will do everything in our power to see to it that our children grow up healthy, secure, and loved. Until then, I think we can look on the age of reason as a stage toward which humanity in the twentieth century is at best slowly moving.

In this passage from the *Confessions,* as a pioneer in the evolution of consciousness, Augustine is implying that each of us is still evolving, and that we shouldn't get bogged down too long in the thinking process. This is a revolutionary concept. Isn't it Einstein who says that the highest mode of knowing is the mystical? Great geniuses in many fields have had some access to the mystical mode of knowing; that is why they were able to leap over accepted conceptual thinking and make tremendous discoveries. With the practice of spiritual disciplines, such moments of insight can become permanent states of awareness. The source of abiding wisdom is within each one of us, waiting to be discovered so it can inform our lives. But we need to keep evolving toward that wisdom, which requires tireless effort.

With spiritual wisdom comes a tremendous realization: there is no joy in anything that is only for oneself. Private satisfaction ends almost as soon as it begins. This is what we discover when we dive into the deepest realms of consciousness, where joy resides. In virtually every field of human activity we can see people chasing some temporary pleasure, admitting that it is not what they expected, and then going on to chase the same will-o'-the-wisp in some other form while life ebbs away. Clinging like this to what is limited and temporary, the mystics tell us, is the cause of all our sorrow.

We can extend this diagnosis to the level of nations. Any country that tries to find security without contributing to the security of the whole globe is bound to find itself riddled with insecurity, one characteristic sign of which is the insane arms race we see so many nations trapped in today. All we have to do is read the newspaper to see this law being borne out in every area of the globe.

Wherever we have a tendency to quarrel, to turn

resentful, to demand equal opportunities for pleasure and profit, the door to the deeper realms of joy is shut. I would even go to the extent of saying that the door to lasting health is shut. We need to remind ourselves of this every day, and one simple way to do so is by repeating the Holy Name. We can use the innumerable bits and pieces of time during the course of even a very busy day to keep fresh this remembrance that the joy of all is my supreme joy; private pleasure at the expense of others is my supreme pain. Living in a civilization where this concept is seldom put forward, we need to keep this reminder before us as often as possible.

Teresa of Avila has given us a simple secret for putting this recipe for joy into action: *Amor saca amor,* "Love begets love." When you live or work with a person who is always loving, even when opposing you, slowly you start changing for the better. To become like this, you have to learn to step aside and get yourself out of the way. That is the secret of perfect relations, of perfect love. *God is love* is an aphorism that expresses the highest of spiritual truths. If we want this divine state to be ours right here on earth, during this very lifetime, we have to work assiduously to remove from our consciousness everything that is private, separate, and self-centered.

Without a sincere effort to get ourselves out of the way, we can't understand the needs of the people closest to us; we can't even see them clearly. Often, for example, even good parents have goals for their children that their children do not share, goals that may not be in anyone's best interests. Here I have to pay a tribute to my grandmother, who never heard of educational psychology – or, for that matter, of any other kind of psychology. The summer I finished high school, living as I did as part of a rather large clan, I was barraged by opinions – from uncles, aunts, brothers-in-law, sisters-in-law, everybody – about what I ought to do with the rest of my life. The only person who didn't try to put pressure on me was my grandmother; she kept her counsel to herself. But at the very end of summer vacation, as I was taking leave of my family to go off to college, she called me over to her and whispered in my ear, "Follow your own star."

To love completely, it is not enough if we care deeply; we must also be detached from ourselves. To know what is best for someone, I have to be able to step aside from my own prejudices and preconceptions, slip into that person's shoes, and become one with him temporarily, looking at life through his eyes rather than my own. When I step back again, I will have seen his needs from the inside; only then can I see clearly how to serve those needs with detachment and compassion. This does not mean conniving at weaknesses he may have; it means that through constant love and support, I can help him to correct those weaknesses. This is the path, the strait and narrow path, that leads to real love.

꧁

Why do we find it so desperately difficult to get ourselves out of the way?

Augustine began by asking us, "Imagine if all the tumult of the body were to quiet down, along with all our busy thoughts. . . ." Every private urge we have can be expressed in terms of noise. A craving for french fries whispers to us urgently in, say, five decibels; a thirst for a cocktail, in ten decibels. Resentment's rasping voice reaches some fifty decibels, and the demands of the ego himself drown out all other sounds. We have innumerable urges like this speaking up continually, and the more often we give in, the louder they cry. It adds up to a tremendous lot of noise.

In fact, I think the mind must be more noisy than the runway of an international airport. Cumbersome urges are landing on our sense-ways at all hours, screeching to a halt at our mind-gates. Desires are taking off continually on flights of hoped-for satisfaction. Huge jet cravings zoom through the skies, breaking the sound barrier. I remember a British advertisement for the Concorde flight from New York to London: "You'll reach your destination before you take off." That kind of promise might have been penned by the ego.

In talking about stillness of mind, Augustine is trying to let us in on one of the most closely guarded secrets of human existence: if all these thought-planes, incoming and outgoing, could be grounded even for a few moments, we would hear the marvelous music that is going on inside always.

One summer many years ago a friend took me on an excursion to Yosemite National Forest, which must be one of the most spectacular in this country. But by the time evening fell there were so many radios going, in campers and out around campfires, that I wondered to myself, "Why did we have to come so far just to hear the same old noise?" Only when the radio-listeners fell asleep and the radios were silenced did I hear the music of a tiny stream, babbling along only a few yards from our campsite. It had been running on all that time, but in the midst of the hubbub I hadn't even known it existed. Its song was so glorious at that moment that it seemed to me almost as if the stream were singing, "I may come and I may go, but the Lord goes on forever."

On the strength of my own experience in meditation, I can assure you that a divine stream of wisdom is flowing in your heart always. When the mind is quietened, you can hear it running blissfully through the very depths of consciousness. As you listen to this song carefully, with complete concentration, from somewhere comes a soft whisper of unshakable certitude: "You are not a finite creature, a separate fragment that one day will pass away. You are infinite and whole, and you will never die." I don't think any greater assurance can come to a human being.

Augustine describes marvelously his own step-by-step descent to this seabed of consciousness:

Thus by stages I passed from bodies to the soul which uses the body for its perceiving, and from this to the soul's inner power, to which the body's senses present external things; and from there I passed on to the reasoning power, to which is referred for judgment what is received from the body's senses. This too realized that it was mutable in me, and rose to its own understanding. It withdrew my thought from its habitual way, abstracting from the confused crowds of phantasms that it might find what light suffused it, when with utter certainty it cried aloud that the immutable was to be preferred to the mutable, and how it had come to know the immutable itself. Thus in the thrust of a trembling glance my mind arrived at That Which is. Then indeed I saw clearly thy "invisible things which are understood by the things that are made."

At this level of awareness the external world is far, far away. You have traveled to an enormous depth, and you know with certainty that this world to which you have descended is much more real, and what you understand at this depth much more valid, than what you see on the surface. On the surface, for example, we feel that it is natural for people to quarrel, for nations to go to war. "It's only human," we say. Now we realize in the depths of our soul that quarreling and fighting are not natural at all. What is natural is loving everybody, seeing everybody as one.

After this experience, even if another person is

offensive or uncooperative, we will easily be able to hear the music of the Lord above the discordant notes of the ego. This is one very practical way in which this supreme discovery can help us in our day-to-day work and relationships. Awareness of this unnamed voice gives you faith in people, and that faith enables them to see themselves in a much more positive light: as a spark of divinity, with undiscovered resources of love, wisdom, and security.

The joy that accompanies this realization of unity is so tremendous that if it were to come upon us suddenly, the nervous system would not be able to bear it. Fortunately it takes many, many years for ordinary people like you and me to reach this state. Even some of the greatest of mystical figures have been physically immobilized for days and nights by the impact of this joy. John of the Cross gives us a taste of its intensity by likening it to the rapture of a tryst between two lovers. Here are the concluding stanzas of his poem "In a Dark Night," which distills in lyric language the course of meditation:

> In a dark night,
> Inflamed with love's impatient longing
> – Oh what good fortune! –
> I went out unseen,
> My house being now all silent;
> . . .
> I lost and forgot myself,
> My face resting on my Beloved;

All things ceased, and I surrendered myself,
Leaving my cares
Forgotten among the lilies.

It takes many years for us to build up our nervous system, our emotional endurance, so that we can receive the impact of these waves of pure joy and still carry on our daily responsibilities. For the world can ill afford to be deprived of the precious contribution such a person can make. This is the underlying purpose of the various disciplines I have been describing to you: first to make this divine experience possible, and then to allow us to function beautifully in everyday life once this experience has been attained. This stream of joy is flowing forever in your consciousness and mine. If anybody asks, "Then why don't I hear it myself?" Augustine gives the answer: the noise of our physical urges and the agitation of the mind is drowning it out. "Be still," the Bible says, "and know that I am God." Augustine, when he finally discovered this joy lying hidden within him, exclaimed,

Late have I loved thee, O Beauty so ancient and so new; late have I loved thee! For behold, thou wert within me and I outside; and I sought thee outside and in my unloveliness fell upon these lovely things that thou hast made. Thou wert with me and I was not with thee. I was kept from thee by those things, yet had they not been in thee, they would not have been at all. Thou didst call and cry to me and break open my deafness; and thou didst send forth thy

beams and shine upon me and chase away my
blindness; thou didst breathe fragrance upon me,
and I drew in my breath and do now pant for thee.
I tasted thee, and now hunger and thirst for thee;
thou didst touch me, and now I burn for thy peace.

Augustine is expressing one of the most joyful real-
izations we can make on the spiritual journey: it is the
Lord alone who all along has been subtly drawing our
attention ever deeper within. Sometimes he uses the
magnetic pull of love, which is naturally the way we
prefer to be drawn toward perfection. But sometimes,
when we do not respond, he must resort to the cor-
rective pressure of pain and sorrow.

In the end, however we are led, none of us will be
able to resist the overwhelming power of the Lord: his
wisdom, his love, his joy, his peace. But through meditation and its allied disciplines, by "straining beyond
ourselves," each of us can make this epic journey
infinitely shorter and sweeter.

[4]

And imagine if that moment were to go on and on, leaving behind all other sights and sounds but this one vision which ravishes and absorbs and fixes the beholder in joy, so that the rest of eternal life were like that moment of illumination which leaves us breathless. . . .

Now we are going to hear, from the mouths of mystics who have experienced it for themselves, just what effects the realization of God wrought on their daily lives. Buried in their accounts somewhere must be hidden the key to the mysterious transformation of their lives – the key that enabled them, according to their own times and temperaments, to bring the joy, the wisdom, and the absorbing peace of that eternal inner realm to bear in this fragmented world. These precious accounts must hold many clues that we, in our round of mundane activities, can apply in our efforts to make our lives a gift to those around us.

Augustine emphasizes that the cacophony of physical and mental urges has to be quieted before we can hear the eternal stream within us. Saint Teresa of Avila, who wrote openly and in detail of her interior experiences, calls this the Prayer of Quiet. "This true Prayer of Quiet has in it an element of the supernatural." Those who experience it, she means, are no longer ordinary. In some sense they have become extraordinary, in that they have connected their body, their mind, and – most important – their will to the divine will within. She goes on:

We cannot, in spite of all our efforts, procure it for ourselves. It is a sort of peace in which the soul establishes herself, or rather in which God establishes the soul. All her powers are at rest. She understands, but otherwise than by the senses, that she is already near her God, and if she draws a little nearer, she will become by union one with him. One feels a great bodily comfort, a great satisfaction of the soul. Such is the happiness of the soul in seeing herself close to the spring, that even without drinking of the waters she finds herself refreshed.

Here we encounter a subtle attitude that seems to set the mystics apart. "We cannot, in spite of all our efforts, procure this for ourselves; it is a sort of peace . . . in which God establishes the soul." Augustine voices the same attitude: "Far be it from me, O Lord, to think that I am happy for any or every joy that I may have. For there is a joy which is not given to the ungodly but only to those who love thee for thy own sake, whose joy is thyself." This joy is a gift – and there is no other way to come by it.

Teresa concludes her description with these ecstatic lines:

It seems to [the soul] that she wants nothing more. Indeed, to those who are in this state it seems that at the least movement [of the mind], they will lose this sweet peace. They are in the palace close to their

King, and they see that he is beginning to give them his kingdom. It seems to them that they are no longer in this world.

They find themselves in the realm of love, they say wonderingly: the realm of reality. Their bodies continue to function in this phenomenal world of ours, but their center no longer lies in a world subject to change and decay, to sorrow and suffering. It is, as Augustine so graphically puts it, fixed in permanent joy.

Yet a great dilemma still presents itself: how are we to cultivate this attitude of theirs until God himself is pleased to grant us the experience they describe?

"It seems that at the least movement" of the mind, Teresa says, "they will lose this sweet peace." This is a formidable clue. When you dive into the deeper realms of consciousness you realize what a noisy factory the mind is, churning out thoughts day in and day out. Most of us are unaware how abrasive this activity is; we have never tasted the healing silence of the world within. Like those who live in the flight paths of a big international airport, we say, "What noise?" We simply don't hear. When I read about people who enjoy scenes of cruelty in movies, for instance, what I hear them saying is that nothing registers of the turmoil in the mind. They have turned their sensitivity to OFF.

Go to a wilderness area, where the sounds of civilization do not reach, and you will understand how great is the contrast between the surface level of awareness and these deeper realms. The silence seems magnified by comparison – and, by the same token, much more eloquent. I suspect this is one of the strongest reasons why city-dwellers take every opportunity to "get away from it all." They relish the chance to escape the noise around them, and to quiet a little the din inside.

Ultimately, however, there is only one place where you and I can find rest: in the depths of our consciousness. Everywhere else we wander is not our true home. I can tell you truthfully that within reason, I have tasted every legitimate satisfaction life has to offer. That is why I would have no hesitation in standing on any platform in the world and saying, "There is no comparison between the joy I find in the depths of my heart and everything I knew before."

Teresa describes in unforgettable words the consolation this experience brings:

> Rapture is a great help to recognize our true home and to see that we are pilgrims in this life. It is a great thing to see what is going on in our home, and to know where we are someday going to live. For if a person has to go and settle in another country, it is a great help to him in undergoing the fatigues of his

journey that he has discovered it to be a country where he may live still, in the most perfect peace.

Augustine addresses his Lord in strikingly similar terms:

> Nor in all these things that my mind traverses in search of you, do I find any sure place for my mind save in you: in whom all that is scattered in me is brought into one, so that nothing of me may depart from you. And sometimes you admit me to a state of mind that I am not ordinarily in, a kind of delight which could it ever be made permanent in me, would be hard to distinguish from the life to come.

Yet the hard fact is that this is but a flash of delight, as he says, a brief moment of wisdom and utter peace. It cannot be sustained for long. It fades. "So I returned to my old habits," Augustine says, "bearing nothing with me but a memory of delight and a desire, as if for something of which I had caught the fragrance but which I had not yet the strength to eat."

Even after you have this ineffable experience, it seems, years of arduous endeavor still lie ahead before your glimpse of the divine can be made permanent. In the depths of meditation you may experience the Prayer of Quiet for a few moments – the space of an *Ave Maria,* as Teresa puts it. But the state to be aimed at, in which that moment of joy goes "on and on," is having this supreme stillness in your heart with your eyes wide open and your senses alert, in the midst of the hurly-burly of daily existence.

Meister Eckhart has a picturesque yet comprehensive way of describing how this miracle of miracles was worked in him: "I was made all of one piece by you, my most sweet God." Wherever you cut the God-conscious person, he says, you will find him the same. Working or playing, with people or alone, awake or asleep, he will be aware of the unity underlying life. This is the real meaning of that elusive phrase "carrying out the will of God." It means, in effect, that you live in joy always.

Peace of mind, in other words, is not an end in itself. It is a means, a phase in one's spiritual growth, and there is much more growth yet to come. The Prayer of Quiet is a great bridge leading from an uncoordinated life of self-centered activity to a new, unified life of selfless action. With it we leave behind our old world, our old habits of mind, in order to go on to greater, wider worlds of loving work.

⤺

The secret to be gleaned from these accounts is delineated by Augustine himself in a marvelously practical prayer:

Thou dost command faithfulness. And when I knew, as it is said, that no one could be faithful unless God gave it, even this was a point of wisdom: to know whose gift it was. For by faithfulness we are

collected and bound up into unity within
ourself, whereas we had been scattered abroad in
multiplicity. Too little does any man love thee,
who loves some other thing together with thee;
loving it not on account of thee, O thou Love,
who art ever burning and never extinguished!
O Charity, my God, enkindle me! Thou dost
command faithfulness: grant what thou dost
command and then command what thou wilt.

This last is the famous sentence which so startled
the ecclesiastics of Augustine's time. What he is saying
is revolutionary: that true faithfulness to the will of
God can only arise out of some personal experience –
in the form of a gift – of its unrivalled power, which
can come only when we have reduced our self-will
almost to zero.

This kind of assertion is common from mystics. It
sets them apart. Yet understandably enough, it gives
rise to grave misgivings among those who would like
to arrive at this faith but have not had the personal
experience that validates it. "Can we not have true
faith," they wonder, "unless it is given to us? What
then is the point of all this effort and self-sacrifice
which is put before us as the way to reach God?"

My answer would be simple: every ounce of effort
makes it that much easier for the experience to be
given to us. Everything we do matters. Meditating
matters very much; so does remembering to repeat
the Holy Name. Working hard and selflessly, eating
nutritious food in moderate quantities, getting

enough exercise, staying calm and kind through the problems of the day: all these matter a good deal. They are, in fact, our real job in life; our other activities are secondary.

On questionnaires we are often asked who our employer is. Each of us is really Self-employed: employed by our innermost Self, the Lord. When we waste time in idle pursuits, when we quarrel, the Lord tries to remind us that we are doing all this on company time: time that belongs to everybody. Isn't your pay docked when you do personal things on company time? The same thing happens in life, though we do not usually make the connection. When we do selfish things, we lose some of our vigor, some of our peace of mind. That is the Lord, trying to alert us that we are wasting precious time.

Those most fortunate few who have had direct experience of the unity underlying seemingly separate phenomena immediately make the connection between their thoughts, their actions, and their peace of mind. When Teresa had to justify her course of action to her Church superiors, she didn't say that a careful survey of previous and analogous situations had produced such and such a recommendation, or that UPS delivered a twenty-page computer printout specifying what she was to do. She would say in complete faith, "His Majesty came himself and told me what to do." This is what becoming established in God means: the welfare of the whole speaks to you, direct and urgent. And the tone of the message is not, "The boss phoned a half hour ago; kindly call him back at your leisure." The Lord says, "Teresa, I am talking to *you*. Give me your complete attention." There is a certitude about that voice, a certitude which can baffle a person who is not used to hearing it. Augustine describes this clearly and dramatically:

> And thou didst cry to me from afar: "l am who am." And I heard thee, as one hears in the heart. And there was from that moment no ground of doubt in me: I would more easily have doubted my own life than have doubted that truth is.

What the Lord tells you is simple. To Francis of Assisi it was "Rebuild my church"; to Augustine, a line from Paul. The actual words are not particularly important; the message is clear and universal: "Live for all. Their joy is your joy." After such an experience it does not matter who tells you, "You didn't hear any such thing. This is not true!" As Pascal says, this truth carries its own validity. It is self-evident.

There is no way of describing the effect of these experiences except by referring to one's own life. I do not ascribe much importance to visions and voices; I look at how a person actually lives. If your experience of unity is genuine, you cannot possibly live for yourself alone, because that is the sum and substance of this call: "Live for all. Work for all." And if you say, "What about a vacation once in a while?" the Lord will be blunt: "I'm giving you a lifelong vacation! That ego of yours, which has always been telling you to stand up for your pleasures and fight for your rights, has been put out of his misery. Now, at long last, you can have a real vacation."

When most of your mental hullabaloo has been quietened, you respond easily and immediately to the sanctity of life. Wherever you see it violated, from a very deep level something in you springs into action. The other morning, after a brisk walk on the beach, I had returned to the car and was scraping the sand off my shoes when out of the corner of my eye I saw a cat leap off a sandbank onto a tiny bird. My response was so fast that I nearly succeeded in grabbing that bird out of the cat's mouth before it realized I was there. I didn't blame the cat; that is its nature. Yet I had to try to save that bird: that, after all, is my nature.

Once you have personal experience of the unity of life, your joy will lie in relieving distress wherever you find it. This requires detachment and enormous faith in human goodness. Only the person who has practiced spiritual disciplines regularly can face sorrow over and over with unflagging faith in the divine core of human nature. Yet when attention is unified, you can see straight into the heart of a person; whatever he does, whatever she suffers, you know that core of divinity remains intact.

Some years ago I read that physicists had designed a microscope that can resolve objects as minute as one billionth of an inch. Who can imagine such a thing? Who can even honestly believe that anything so small as an angstrom exists? Yet here are physicists stating confidently that they can observe the atomic structure of almost any solid material. When attention is unified, it has much the same penetrating capabilities. You can observe minute connections linking thoughts and events in the very depths of the unconscious.

Augustine describes for us what he saw when he looked through the microscope of unified attention: ". . . the glory of that ever-fixed eternity in which nothing passes, but the whole is present." And he asks searchingly: "Who shall hold the heart of man, that it may stand still and see how eternity, ever still standing, neither past nor future, utters the times past and to come?"

All of us have this inherent capacity to glimpse eternity; we have it in abundance. But for the most part we direct it towards very limited goals, frittering away its power on things that have scant capacity to satisfy our enormous appetite for joy, unity, and meaning. This misapplication is the root of our frustrations in life. "Why are men not happy?" Augustine asked himself. "Because they are much more concerned over things which are more powerful to make them unhappy than truth is to make them happy, in that they remember truth so slightly."

There is an enormous charge in memory; that is why so many of these mystics frame their statements in terms of time. When you remember an offensive remark that someone dear said ten years ago, you get offended all over again. Imagine how many unpleasant memories of this sort we must have, each with a certain negative charge, lying around in the lower stacks of the library of consciousness. In these archives there are no harmless reports; these memories are more like time bombs ticking away, waiting for a suitable occasion to explode.

Now imagine, if you will, a state of mind in which you have defused the pain and pleasure charges of every memory in your consciousness. This is one of the operating principles of meditation: if you can bring your mind back to the present every time it wanders away, you will eventually not have to deal with old anxieties at all. Your memories will still be there in the lower stacks, but they will have no hold over you.

I can remember the kind things people have said to me over the years; I remember some of the unkind things too. I remember events that have been good to me and those which have not been so good. But because I keep my attention focused on the present, these memories have no more charge. That is the real answer to problems of anxiety about the past, with its selfish attachments and ridiculous mistakes. It is equally the remedy for those otherwise inevitable fears for the future. When the mind becomes one-pointed, focused like a laser, its immense power is not diffused by anxiety or fear. You can use it effectively for lifting the burden of past and future, and for helping others to lift these burdens too.

This is not repression. When you repress a potent

memory, you make it stronger. You have forced it below the conscious level of awareness, but although it is out of sight there, it commands more attention than ever. What I am talking about is the skill of withdrawing attention from any moment but the present. When you can do that, the emotional charge of a memory is not suppressed and hidden; it simply evaporates. What gives memories and fears power over us is their capacity to soak up our attention; when that capacity goes, their burden falls away.

Even one glimpse of deepest awareness has enormous practical repercussions. In these moments of peace your vital organs and nervous system rest, and even though it may last only a short while, the quality of that rest is of the highest. You come back into the phenomenal world refreshed, recharged, invigorated, ready to face any challenge. This makes every day precious, every single hour precious, so that you become almost constitutionally incapable of wasting time now. In a sense you come back a new woman, a new man, with the mandate to use your newly harnessed energy in work that promotes the health, happiness, and harmony of all.

I wish I could find some way to convey the wonder of this. In meditation you can go into a vast treasurehouse inside. You have a kind of latchkey: you can go in anytime and draw out as much as you like. The manager, the Lord, sits there behind his big desk and says, "Go in and help yourself. Stuff your pockets. Only make sure you go back and use it all for others."

That is the agreement, which he has got in writing, so to say, sealed with your very life. Thus meditation works miracles: it recharges your enthusiasm and restores a robust optimism for life. It is the supreme education.

Living on the surface of life as we do, we don't suspect what a treasure trove of love and wisdom we have within. If I knew of a simple, painless way of unlocking this treasure, I would be the first to give it. But as far as I know, there is no way to enter and make use of these untold riches except by practicing meditation and integrating its allied disciplines into our daily life. There is no shortcut around the travail of this journey into consciousness, and those who have traversed it testify that it is the ultimate test of human endurance. Yet this is the very challenge that appeals to people. It banishes boredom and brings the dew of freshness to every day. There can be no failure in this effort: for as you go deeper and deeper into your consciousness, you discover that you have vast resources of which you never dreamed: resources with which to help yourself, to help your family and community, to contribute to your society, to change the very world for the better. The unending miracle of these resources is that they are there within every one of us. We have only to dive deep to discover them.

So it is this we can all aim for: not having mystical experiences, but making our life a gift to the members of our family and our society, just as it has been given as a gift to us. If spiritual experiences do come our way, they will serve to inspire us and further fuel our efforts. Here I am realistic enough to recognize that most of us have drawbacks and failings that stand between us and this loftiest of goals. That is why I appreciate it when people say, "Don't talk philosophy to me. Don't talk about sweetness and light. Tell me precisely what meditation can do to help me: one, two, three, four, five."

I respond very favorably to this businesslike approach. I reply, "I too am a man who means business. My business is the same as everybody else's business: learning to live in love and act in wisdom, at home and at work, with people we like and with people we don't like too." Money plays no part in this kind of business. Material possessions, prestige, power over others, have no role whatever. You can observe people at the highest levels of success; in the home life of the most respected politicians, the most eminent scientists, the most inspired artists, and the most effective businessmen you will find the same human problems: conflicts, anger, frustration, disappointment, depression. Their lives do have a bright side, but they make it clear that neither money nor prestige nor power can enable us to make our life a gift worth giving.

What meditation can do, gradually, is nothing less than re-educate our very habits of mind, so that we can respond to difficult times and difficult people with patience, resourcefulness, and compassion. It can teach us to respect opposition when we meet with it, evaluate it with detachment, and hold true to our convictions with kindness and persuasion if they stand the test. These are great arts in the field of living, which every one of us can learn through meditation.

For me, the selfish person is simply uneducated. The stubborn, self-centered person is ignorant of the most elementary skill in life – the skill of living in harmony with others. Just as people can be taught to read and write so well that they can someday compose poetry or dash off persuasive, cogent reports, we can teach our mind to respond the way we want it to respond. That is the long and the short of meditation. Impatient people can learn to become patient. Those with a history of crippling insecurities can learn to be secure. Those who are lethargic can make themselves energetic in their efforts to serve a worthy cause. Those who are self-centered can learn to widen their sphere of concern to include more individuals than themselves. There is no greater curriculum than these skills, no finer art, no more useful science.

For a reading list in this curriculum, we have the accounts of the mystics of every major religious tradition, whose experience of the eternal, when everything is said and done, is the same. Reading these accounts is an important step in spiritual education, for there is much to unlearn in the conditioning of the mass media. But no amount of reading can enable us to change ourselves; contrary habits of mind are

twelve-year-old tries out some highly contemporary sarcasm on you, he is administering a midterm; when your partner seems bent on provoking a full-scale verbal war over the scrambled eggs, that is a final exam. Finals are tough; you can't expect them to be a cinch. If everybody got an A, the lesson wouldn't be worth learning. But if you pass, you don't dare pat yourself on the back; bigger tests are sure to be around the corner. Whatever your domestic scene, you can look on it as a tough prep school for learning how to practice the words you meditate on every morning and evening.

One essential part of this lesson is time. I have to repeat this because in the breakneck pace of our age it is so easily forgotten. I am always surprised at how little time people spend together in many homes today. Rushing out to beat the competition to a few extra dollars seems to enjoy higher priority than does learning the basic skills of living. In the long run, by getting our values turned around, we pay an awful price. Nothing in the world is worth the expense of forgetting how to live. What use is a fortune – even if you win it, which is scarcely assured – once you have forgotten how to live?

I used to counsel people, "Why don't you get up a little earlier – even if it means going to bed a little earlier! – so you can spend a little more time with your family or friends in the morning and get the day off to a happy start?" In an atmosphere of frenzied friction, even the finest meal will turn to ashes. The person who starts the day with a peaceful, happy breakfast is likely to be a better stenographer, a better doctor, a better librarian, a better scientist, a better friend.

When you arrive at work, that too is a good time to remember the words of your meditation: "Make me an instrument of thy peace." It takes all kinds to make up an office or shop or classroom. What the miracle of meditation promises is simple: of course it takes all sorts, but you can learn to work in harmony with every sort imaginable – especially since what prevents us from working in harmony is usually no more than lack of patience.

When a person has difficulty working with others, you have only to scrutinize his behavior to hear his mind saying, "These people don't know anything! Why don't they pay attention to me?" Patience decrees that we be ready and willing to learn from anyone. An open attitude disarms everybody; that is its charm – and its magic. "Here is someone who is willing to listen," we say to ourselves. "Maybe I can pick up a few things from him too." It is as simple as that. After all, our life can't begin to be a gift until others are willing to receive it.

Sometimes I hear people complain, "Oh, in my job I've got to go on filing from morning till night. I never get to do anything challenging." What is as important as the job we do is how we do it, how well we can work in harmony with those around us – which, for most of us, is challenge enough. This is especially true of work done in service to others. The way violence is escalating today, both in our streets and around the globe, I don't think there is any limit to the value of work done in the spirit of harmony and peace. We may not be great figures on the world stage, we may not hold a job that shows spectacular results, but the world cannot afford to lose the contribution of anyone who is working for forgiveness, harmony, and tolerance, even if only on a small scale. Any such work is a precious gift.

When we look with sensitivity at the life of Jesus, bringing comfort and consolation to millions of people, I think most of us say to ourselves at some level, "How I would like to be like that in some small measure!" In his early days as Francesco Bernardone, the cloth merchant's son, Saint Francis was not a particularly spiritual figure. Neither was young Augustine in the days when he was painting Carthage red. What overwhelmed them, as it has overwhelmed hundreds of other seekers who went on to become towering spiritual figures, was this immense desire to remake themselves in the image of Jesus.

Even ordinary people like you and me can dedicate ourselves to this loftiest of endeavors; and when we do so earnestly, our body begins to glow with health, our mind becomes gradually more and more secure, our intellect grows more lucid, our will becomes unbreakable, and our life becomes a gift to everybody who looks on it with an open heart. These are the benefits of taking up the spiritual search in earnest: one, two, three, four, and five.

[5]

*. . . leaving behind all other sights and sounds but
this one vision, which ravishes and absorbs and fixes
the beholder in joy . . .*

I am now going to take up the most valuable
– and probably the most misunderstood – of treasures
that we have: desire. Desire is the fuel we have been
given for this long, arduous journey into the depths of
consciousness. What often makes the journey longer
and more arduous than it need be, if I may say so,
is our tendency to fritter desire away, in an endless
round of pursuits which lead us nowhere.

Spinoza once pointed out succinctly that desires
are not decisions. We have very little choice in them.
Yet desire is raw power, of a magnitude at least as
immense as that of nuclear energy. It is absolutely
incumbent upon all of us to work to harness this
power within us, so that what we do, we decide in freedom.

Once we see desire for what it really is, interestingly
enough, doing something out of purely personal
motives will no longer be pleasant. Doing things with
the desire to help others, on the other hand, will give
us enormous pleasure. With this understanding, the
whole alignment of our desires undergoes a transformation.

Do you remember Augustine declaring, "By faithfulness we are collected and bound up into unity
within ourself, whereas we had been scattered abroad

in multiplicity"? It is this basic change of attitude with respect to desire, more than anything else, that opens up the vast treasury within. By a natural process, our capacity to desire actually grows with our capacity to make our actions a gift to others. Sensory desires, for example, are only nickel-and-dime satisfactions. It is only when we don't have a wider frame of reference than ourselves that we believe they hold out the promise of great pleasure. When we widen our horizons to encompass a greater breadth of life, we can evaluate these pleasures more shrewdly. Some of the greatest of mystics experimented with their senses rather freely in their earlier days. When they reach a state of unlimited compassion and concern for others, they admit, "Those were mere pennies. Now I am in possession of wealth beyond my wildest dreams!"

‍ᴔ

"What happens to sense pleasures, then?" people naturally want to know. "Should we aim to become bleak ascetics?"

"Why is it that I don't see you playing in the sandbox any more?" I ask, by way of answer.

"The sandbox?" they wonder, taken aback. "The sandbox is for kids."

Picture grown-up men and women getting into the sandbox and playing happily for hours together with toy shovels and buckets! That is something like the picture these mystics must get when they see you and me throwing our energy into pursuits as limited as sense pleasures, which run through our fingers like sand. With their vastly wider perspective, they are able to look far down the road and see that the only possible outcome of this kind of play is increasing frustration.

Every human being has been granted a huge reservoir of desire; we all have it in abundance. Measured against this immense reservoir, the senses have a ridiculously limited capacity to satisfy our enormous appetite to know and to love. You remember Augustine's question: "Why are men not happy? Because they are much more concerned over things which are more powerful to make them unhappy than truth is to make them happy, in that they remember truth so slightly." It is the existence of this truth that we need to be reminded of as often as possible.

When I hear adults, who should know better, going around complaining, "I want all the pleasures of the senses that I enjoyed in my teens," I would like to put before them the example of my young friend Jessica. It wasn't very long ago that I saw her playing with dolls. I understand there are dolls now which, if you press a button, actually get a fever. Perfect for playing hospital! But Jess has graduated from dolls to people. She has worked hard to become an accomplished nurse, and now she is helping and comforting real patients. In the same way, now that we are grown up, our joy should consist in helping others. Once we so much as taste this joy, we will feel no need to play at being children again.

When I use the word love in this connection, I do so advisedly; the popular sense of the word tends to be superficial. I use it in the deeply spiritual sense, where to love is to know; to love is to act. If you really love, from the depths of your consciousness, that love will give you a native wisdom. "When what is known, if even so little, is loved," Augustine writes beautifully, "this very capacity for love makes it better and more fully known." With this capacity you perceive the needs of others intuitively and clearly, with detachment from any personal desires; and you know how to act creatively to meet those needs, dexterously surmounting any obstacle that comes in the way. Such is the immense, driving power of love.

Great mystics like Augustine and Teresa take this one relentless step further. If you really love, they ask, how can you act selfishly? They find it impossible to waste a day, even an hour, that could be used for helping others. For spiritual giants like these, in other words, to love is to act.

Mystics resort to the language of love often. They know that the Lord is the true fulfillment of our deepest need to love. This is a certitude stamped with their personal experience, and it sometimes strikes me that they are dying to share with us this crucial secret. Augustine speaks to his Lord with direct passion in the *Confessions,* calling on him as "God of my heart," "God, my sweetness," and "O my late joy!" God has become the focus to which he directs all his love, thus magnifying its intensity immeasurably. "This is happiness," he tells us: "to be joyful in thee and because of thee: this and no other."

Then he gives a devastating diagnosis of our failures in love:

> ...Yet the reason may be that what they cannot do they do not want to do with sufficient intensity to make them able to do it.

Each of us wants abiding joy. We want it more than anything. Yet we can find abiding joy, Augustine is telling us, only in loving with all our heart, with all our will. All our time and all our energy must be caught up in this all-consuming effort to love. A person like Augustine ultimately fills himself to bursting with this one uplifting desire, so that he floats free from the need to try constantly to satisfy a hundred and one smaller desires. Every cell of his being fills with this love, "which ravishes and absorbs and fixes the beholder in joy."

"Love desires to be aloft," Thomas a Kempis exclaims exuberantly in his *Imitation of Christ*, "and will not be kept back by any thing low and mean. . . . He that loveth, flyeth, runneth, and rejoiceth; he is free, and cannot be held in." Augustine tries to give us some way of grasping this great joy, if only vaguely, by comparing it to more self-centered pleasures:

> But what is it that I love when I love You? Not the beauty of any bodily thing, nor the order of seasons, not the brightness of light that rejoices the eye, nor the sweet melodies of all songs, nor the sweet

fragrance of flowers and ointments and spices, not manna or honey, not the limbs that carnal love embraces. None of these things do I love in loving my God.

Yet in a sense I do love light and melody and fragrance and food and embrace when I love my God: the light and the voice and the fragrance and the food and embrace in the soul, when that light shines upon my soul which no place can contain, that voice sounds which no time can take from me, I breathe that fragrance which no wind scatters, I eat the food which is not lessened by eating, and I lie in the embrace which satiety never comes to sunder. This it is that I love when I love my God.

It is exercise that helps this great love grow inside us. It is giving in to anger and jealousy and resentment that stunts it and holds us, with their heavy weight of turmoil and conflict, down on the ground. Most of the advice the mystics give us aims to promote one thing: the exercise of our love. If we do not understand this purpose, their advice can sound platitudinous – or worse still, quite mad.

If there ever was a spiritual madcap, it was Jesus the Christ. "Bless them that curse you. Do good to them that hate you and despitefully use you." People must have rushed back to Jerusalem shouting, "There's a madman loose on some mountaintop, telling us to love our enemies!" It is in Saint Francis of Assisi that we can see the attitude Jesus wants us to take up: "Lord, keep me floating in the empyrean of love for you, so that I cannot even remember to bump against others with my self-will. When I begin to sink back down under my own weight, have the mercy to give me an enemy or two on whom I can practice my love!" This is the kind of daring on which love thrives.

In this sense, the lovers of God never allow themselves to sober up. With ceaseless practice, they keep themselves drunk with the spirit of love day and night. When we have the privilege of hearing about their exploits or reading their intoxicating words, we say to ourselves: "I want to get into this tavern too! I want to sit on that high stool and say to the Divine Bartender, 'The usual, please. A double shot of sympathy, on the rocks.'" We look dazedly and see, perched on stools all around, the men and women of God. There is Teresa, holding tight to the bar to keep from floating away. There is Francis, hardly able to utter his favorite prayer, "My God and my all." There is Augustine, murmuring something about "God, my sweetness." This mysterious joy that knows no limits is our true heritage, the fulfillment that the travail of human evolution is urging.

When we practice meditation with all the enthusiasm we are capable of, when we repeat the name of the Lord, and most of all when we work harmoniously with difficult people and remain kind and respectful in the midst of provocation, we are drinking deep of the Lord's healing mercy. I sometimes see stickers on cars, proclaiming, "God loves you." God is love. He can be nothing else. When we work to live up to this supreme ideal of charity, we become conduits for his love, instruments of his peace. This is what is meant by God's forgiveness: when we embody his love, we will not be capable of doing anything that causes sorrow to another creature.

In the depths of our heart the Lord is pleading: "Come close and look at me, come deeper and deeper and become one with me, and you will be blessed wherever you go." We may think our heart is hungry for success, hungry for pleasure, but the mystics assure us, "Oh, no! What your heart is hungering for, what everyone's heart is hungering for, is the revelation that our real personality is divine."

⊷

The great doubt that comes to everybody is: "I don't know how to do this. I don't really think I can love that way." Here the miracle of love comes in.

If you look at popular novels, at gossip magazines, at syrupy soap operas and movies, you come away with the impression that falling in love is something that just happens. Here you are, sauntering down Fourth Street minding your own business, when suddenly you spy a certain someone coming out of a shop and you fall in love as if into a manhole. True love is much harder to come by than that.

The mystics are the world's authorities on love. When Saint Teresa says *"Amor saca amor,"* she is giving us the basic principle: "Love begets love." One of the most beautiful things about love is that even today it cannot be purchased. It cannot be stolen, it cannot be ransomed, it cannot be cajoled, it cannot be seduced. *Amor saca amor:* only genuine love begets love.

All of us have been conditioned, even though we may not put it in such crass terms, to believe that if you love me six units, I should love you at most six units in return. I can feel secure in loving you six units because you have already committed yourself that far. But if you get annoyed with me and stomp out, slamming the door, I should get annoyed in return – and pull back, at least temporarily, my six units of love. This is the type of bargain that more and more so-called lovers strike today. Saint Teresa would say uncompromisingly, "Don't pretend that this is love. It falls more accurately under the heading of commerce." Shakespeare put the matter in perfect perspective: "Call it not love that changeth."

The whole thrust of what Teresa is confiding to us is simple: With practice, everyone can learn to love like this; everyone can live in endless love. After all, even if you don't learn Esperanto, your life is not necessarily going to be dull and drab. Even if you are not intimately acquainted with ancient Sumerian sculpture, you can make it through life without suffering serious depression. But – and this has to be drilled into the ears of the modern world – if you do not learn how to love, everywhere you go you are going to suffer.

Even in the wealthiest home, discord can leave the

members bankrupt. Ask people who "have it all": several luxury cars in the circular drive, large-screen satellite TV setups in every bedroom and den, heated pools and saunas and exercise machines, priceless originals scattered casually throughout the house. If they live in disharmony, they will be the first to admit, "Life is miserable. I wake up in the morning dreading to go to the breakfast table. I come back in the evening with a sinking feeling in my heart." These are the simple facts of life.

One trend I see which only focuses domestic disharmony is competition. "How much money does he bring in? How much does she bring in?" We should divide up our chattels and responsibilities fair and square, legal-minded advisors warn us, even to the "ownership" of our children. Millions of people have absorbed this criterion. The real question to keep asking ourselves is, "How much am I making my life worthy of being a gift?" Saint Francis says perfectly, "It is in giving that we receive." Right on, as my young friends would say. What matters is not who brings in more or invests more or inveigles more; it is who gives more. That person is the real provider, the true light of the home.

Children, likewise, can exercise their love. When they find their parents slowly moving apart, they can help bring them together with their love. Where grandparents are squabbling, parents can work to reestablish peace. Everybody can learn to play this great mediating role. I know of no greater gift.

⊸

Still, practicing this kind of love is not easy. After I give a talk people sometimes come up to me distraught and tell me: "But you don't know the atmosphere in my home! You haven't met my office mates!"

I hasten to assure them, "You don't have to give me the details. I wasn't raised in a cave." I grew up in a large joint family, where we couldn't escape rubbing shoulders with one another at every turn. Later I worked on campuses with thousands of students, and must have attended hundreds of meetings where faculty members from all departments often differed with each other with passionate conviction. I am perfectly well aware that in every context there can be people who are difficult – every bit as difficult as we ourselves can be at times. Wherever we turn in life, we are liable to run into challenging predicaments.

When I was teaching on university campuses, however, I was also practicing meditation and trying to translate the teachings of the mystics into my daily life. Gradually I learned to cease looking upon challenges as difficulties, and began to see tense situations as opportunities to put my growing love to use. We can do this everywhere; the family context is perfect.

In every family, for example, there is likely to be somebody with a bit of Jonathan Swift. Swift, you know, had a sardonic tongue and a rather black sense of humor; he is said to have worn mourning on his birthday. This sort of thing has an inhibiting effect on everyone, and naturally enough, when the Jonathan of our own family enters the room, others may try to make themselves scarce. Not the person who is trying to take love seriously. She learns to come up with a genuine smile and says, "Come in, Jonathan! I've been looking forward to seeing you." To herself she can add in a whisper, "I need the opportunity to deepen my patience."

As we become more aware that the same spark of divinity is in all of us, we will find opportunities everywhere to make that divinity more evident. We won't see anybody as an enemy; we will see everybody as a friend. Every event, however difficult or potentially threatening, can be used to help carry out what the mystics call "the will of the Lord": to love, to forgive, to be kind.

In other words, these are daily exercises, very much like aerobics. You don't stop when your heart rate gets up to 85. You say, "My target rate is 120," and you keep at it until you get there. When your heart is accustomed to 120, you can start aiming for 130, then for 140. Where physical conditioning is concerned, everybody accepts this process.

It is exactly the same process for increasing patience. The resting rate for patience is zero: you say, "I don't have any patience at all. I blow my stack at the slightest provocation!" I commiserate with such people by patting them on the back and reminding them, "That is where everybody starts." But as you learn to meditate, you get more and more capacity to draw on. After a while, when Jonathan goes out of his way to provoke you, you find you can bear it cheerfully for half an hour. With continuing practice, you reach the point where you can get through an entire Saturday morning without losing control. From seven-thirty until noon, you are so patient that you begin to relish your show of self-mastery. After lunch – wisely, I would say – you make yourself scarce again, because your patience has run dry. But if you keep at it with the same diligence in every arena of personal affairs, the great day arrives when you can be patient around poor Jonathan throughout the weekend. He does his level best to provoke you, but you say to yourself, "Oh, no, you don't! Those days are over. Nowadays I can be patience itself."

There is a remarkable statement in mysticism which I am now going to translate into the language of learning to love. Through sheer exercise, over a long, long period, we do not just love Jonathan or Josephine; we become love itself. Our love radiates to anyone who comes within our orbit; we simply lose the knack of doing otherwise. It does not matter whether the person seated beside us has been unpleasant to us for years, perhaps has even opposed us; that is immaterial. What matters is that our very nature now is love. At all times, in every situation, we are at our best with everybody. This is the answer to our most profound prayers.

We need to stretch the frontiers of this miracle as

far as we can. To me, any person who even thinks about waging war — economics and politics completely aside — needs desperately to learn how to love. Saint Teresa's principle "Love begets love" does not apply only to personal relationships; it works on the level of nations just as well. Here again, Saint Francis is a marvelous teacher. How do we make ourselves into instruments of world peace? How can we forge our nation into an instrument of world peace? Francis replies, "Where there is hatred, let me sow love; where there is injury, pardon." He does not mean it as an incantation for special state occasions; it is given to us as a dynamic exercise.

I have enjoyed the opportunity of wandering through a good number of countries. Everywhere I made the same discovery: what divides one people from another is just one percent of superficial differences; in the other ninety-nine percent, we are all the same.

On my way to this country from India, I spent a week in Paris with other Fulbright scholars. My friends were intent on catching glimpses of the Louvre, the Eiffel Tower, the Left Bank, and (I suspect, though they spared me the details) the Folies-Bergère. I spent my days in the lovely city parks, watching French children happily at play. "Just exactly like Indian children," I used to say to myself. "Where is the difference?" On my return to India I was invited to speak before many groups, and always I was asked searching questions about the United States. I could see that they looked on this continent as another world, and Americans as a different kind of people. Imagine their surprise when I responded, "They're the same as you and me. People there like to be treated kindly, just like people here."

Today doubts about the future of mankind are part of the emotional atmosphere. I feel dispirited when I hear that young people, confronted with hard choices in their lives, are saying more and more often: "What does it matter? By the time I'm grown up, they'll probably have blown the earth sky-high!" Too often these doubts are justified by the actions they see so-called responsible leaders taking. Worldwide, the governments of nations are spending six hundred billion dollars every year on developing and manufacturing weapons of destruction; half a million educated, intelligent scientists are working hard at this task. What is desperately needed are personal examples of another attitude, another way of living.

If we could only remember the simple truth that people everywhere are ninety-nine percent the same and only one percent different, we would be saved a lot of headaches, and we would still have that intriguing one percent to make living a delight. Sometimes I wish a few politicians would take to meditation; then they would find it difficult to overlook the fact that all of us have the same basic needs. We all cherish health, happiness, and love; and we all desire, most important, to live in peace and harmony.

In today's shaky world, believe me, everybody takes hope from you when you have some awareness of the unity of life. Remember Francis's line: "Where there is despair, let me sow hope." Even those who sometimes belittle your efforts cannot help thinking after a while, "This just might show us the way out of our troubles." None of us can afford any longer to think in terms of living just for ourselves, or even of living just for our own family. When you can return good will for ill will, love for hatred, you are restoring the faith of everyone around you in these timeless values. As you begin to take this responsibility seriously, your life slowly takes on the greater meaning that all of us dearly desire.

Giving people grounds for hope is exactly what we are doing when we strive every day to make love the basis of our lives. I read a deeply moving article about a group of peasants in Central America who managed to flee the terror rampant in their homeland by swimming a river into the neighboring country. Sympathetic people from this country are going down to live with them in shifts in an effort to discourage military units from harassing them. The one thing these peasants talk about most is their former archbishop, who, in the face of a brutal civil war, spent his time pleading with his people to lay down their weapons. Though he was assassinated for these efforts, his people will never forget his example. As they say over and over again, in the simplest words imaginable: "He who falls for the people will live in the people."

In this we have an enormous responsibility: to keep in good health, not so much for our own sake but so that we can go on giving this gift as long as possible. Doctors, nurses, and medical technicians can be valuable allies in this sacred task, but the primary responsibility is ours alone. Health is something we have to educate ourselves to maintain, beginning with a nutritious diet, appropriate exercise, work which benefits others, loving relationships, and the enthusiastic observance of spiritual disciplines.

Here I continue a step beyond conventional medicine. In order even to contract illness, I would say, bacteria and viruses and environmental stress are not enough; we must have a certain susceptibility to illness. The immune system is not simply a physiological network, and it is clear that there are wide differences in how different individuals resist disease. Some people exposed to a particular virus get sick; others, though exposed to the same conditions, do not. Similarly, we know that spontaneous remissions – often termed "miraculous" – do occur. All this is because there are many, many factors involved in resistance, and number one, in my opinion, is the mind. The highest, most effective kind of resistance – to illness of any kind whatsoever, even to the ravages of time – is a deep, deep desire to live for others. This is a tremendous force, which I can testify to from my own life.

I am talking now about the deepest roots of the human being. Psychologists know the vital necessity of the will to live; yet when you live only for yourself, how deep can the will go? My will to live springs from the love that floods my heart when I realize that the Lord himself finds it possible to inhabit your heart and mine; and this love expresses itself in the myriad choices I make in my daily life. Most of us have experienced firsthand the benefits we reap from loving two or three people. Imagine what love for five or six billion people can do!

All of us can be much healthier than we are, much more secure. Most of us can live much longer than we expect to, and work more actively right into the evening of our life. Even in our nineties we can be productive, creative, cherished, and respected, because our life has become a shining gift. The time to cultivate the habits of living that make all this possible is now.

↜

> . . . so that the rest of eternal life were like that
> moment of illumination which leaves us breathless.
> Would this not be what is hidden in Scripture,
> "Enter thou into the joy of thy lord"?

For a few rare people, it is not enough to have access to the treasury within. They fall so deeply in love with the President of the bank that they long to know him personally, to live with him forever. Augustine makes this desire understandable for us in a startling story:

> Suppose, brethren, a man should make a ring for his betrothed, and she should love the ring more wholeheartedly than the betrothed who made it for her. . . . Certainly, let her love his gift: but if she should say, "The ring is enough; I do not want to see his face again," what would we say of her? . . . The pledge is given her by the betrothed so that, in his pledge, he himself may be loved. God, then, has given you all these things. Love him who made them.

Even for those fortunate souls who have been given ready access to the treasury within, and who go in at will and stuff their pockets with love, wisdom, energy, and the creative capacity to inspire others to improve their lives, there may still be a massive door deep inside with a gold-plated sign: "Do Not Enter." This intrigues them. They linger outside the door, listening to get some idea of who might be lodged within. Distantly they may hear someone singing *Ave Maria* in a lovely baritone; and more than anything, they long to see the singer with their own eyes.

Once we hear this voice in our heart of hearts, all our desires come together. We take to standing at this door within for hours on end, hoping against hope that one day it will open. We keep on knocking softly, longing for the moment when the voice inside responds, "Come in."

This is the point at which the mystics advise us, "You may have to bring your sleeping bag and camp outside that door for years. You never know when it will open, or even whether it will open at all." Yet if people can camp on the sidewalk for tickets to the World Series, surely we can do as much for the Lord! This is the period when all our loyalty and endurance are tested. For we have it on good authority that the Lord has a one-way window, and although we have not yet glimpsed him face to face, as Paul says, he is watching us continuously to check on the deepest desires of our heart. We have to keep ourselves at our very best each moment; and we have to give our very best, standing ready to love and respect even those who offend us or try to do us wrong. The exercise of love never becomes more daring.

Yet throughout this trying period, we know in our heart of hearts that true and lasting joy is not long off. "She understands," Teresa says of the soul at this stage, "that she is already near her God, and that if she draws a little nearer, she will become by union one with him." We actually find ourselves looking for opportunities to "do good to them who hate us," the more swiftly to enlarge our love.

Finally the huge oaken door opens a crack, hesitates, creaks, then opens a little wider. . . . We stand there holding our breath. For what we see within, in all its breathtaking loveliness, is the Lord himself, our deepest Self, our true divinity. There and then we go beyond time, beyond place, beyond circumstance, beyond change, decay, and death.

> I entered into my own depths, with you as guide; and I was able to do it because you were my helper. I entered, and with the eye of my soul, such as it was, I saw your unchangeable light shining over that same eye of my soul, over my mind. . . . He who knows the truth knows that light, and he that knows the light knows eternity. Love knows it. O eternal truth, true love, beloved eternity!

That is Augustine's on-the-spot, eyewitness account. Later, when he has a chance to put his insights together, he gives us an unforgettable description of his vision:

> What art thou then, my God? O thou, the greatest and the best, mightiest, almighty, most merciful and most just, utterly hidden and utterly present, most beautiful and most strong, abiding yet mysterious, suffering no change and changing all things: never new, never old, making all things new; ever in action, ever at rest, gathering all things to thee and needing none; sustaining and fulfilling and protecting, creating and nourishing and making perfect; ever seeking though lacking nothing. Thou lovest without subjection to passion, thou art jealous but not with fear; thou canst know repentance but not sorrow, be angry yet

unperturbed by anger. Thou canst change
the works thou hast made, but thy mind stands
changeless. Thou dost find and receive back what
thou didst never lose; art never in need but dost
rejoice in thy gains, art not greedy but dost exact
interest manifold. Thou owest nothing yet dost pay
as if in debt to thy creature, forgivest what is owed
to thee yet dost not lose thereby. And with all this,
what have I said, my God and my life and my sacred
delight? What can anyone say when he speaks of
thee?

The illumined man or woman sees divinity in
everyone: the same Lord disguised as billions of
human beings. If you ask me how many people there
are in this country, my truthful answer would have to
be "One." At the customs gate on the entrance to San
Francisco International Airport, I would put up a
subtle sign: "United States of America, Population
One." There are over two hundred fifty million bodies
in this country – two hundred fifty million costumes,
if you like; two hundred fifty million vehicles. Yet
there is only one driver, one wearer, one Self. This
universal vision Augustine posed poetically as the
loftiest of harmonies:

> God is the unchanging conductor as well as the
> unchanged Creator of all things that change.
> When he adds, abolishes, curtails, increases or
> diminishes the rites of any age, he is ordering all
> events according to his providence, until the beauty

of the completed course of time, whose parts are the
dispensations suitable to each different period,
shall have played itself out, like the great melody
of some ineffable composer.

⌁

This vision is within the reach of every
human being. To live in abiding joy and unfailing
love, to serve everyone to the best of our abilities, to
call the whole world our family: this is the magnificent destiny for which the human being is meant.
When the mystic is asked, just as I have been asked
many times, "What is the way by which we can reach
this destiny, claim this legacy, grow to have our head
crowned with the stars?" the reply is simple: "Unify
your desires."

The reward, I can assure you, is worth everything
we can give, every sacrifice we can possibly make.
Catching even a glimpse of this glory will make every
hardship seem slight by comparison. We must strive
to unify all the petty, personal streams of desire that
motivate us until desire for everlasting love surges in
us like a mighty river whose only outlet, whose only
fulfillment, is the sea of love we call the Lord.

In the *Imitation of Christ,* Thomas a Kempis expresses
this longing in a passionate prayer:

> Enlarge thou me in love, that with the inward palate
> of my heart I may taste how sweet it is to love, and to
> be dissolved, and as it were to bathe myself in thy
> love.

Let me be possessed by love, mounting above myself through excessive fervor and admiration.

Let me sing the song of love, let me follow thee, my Beloved, on high; let my soul spend itself in thy praise, rejoicing through love.

Let me love thee more than myself, nor love myself but for thee: and in thee all that truly love thee, as the law of love commandeth, shining out from thyself.

There is a picturesque way of portraying this strange predicament in which we humans find ourselves. Imagine for a moment the Lord standing in the deep vault of the heart, just waiting for us, with all the joy, all the fulfillment we could ever want, calling over and over again, "Come and take it all!" In our congenital deafness, we think the call must be coming from outside. We hear echoes resounding everywhere. Searching them out, one by one, we are more and more confounded not to find the source of the voice. Still it calls to us – in the form of unfulfilled longings.

In the most practical of terms, the fact that the Lord is indeed our deepest, our inmost Self means that we should never give up on ourselves, never give up on anybody on earth. Nobody is lost. The Lord is not going to leave us – indeed, without him there is no life. Even if we have to be dragged home, so to speak, every soul's calling is to be united with him one day. This final, joy-filled homecoming, this reunion, we bring closer every day that we strive to make our life the kind of gift that is worthy of Him whose gift our very life is.

An Eight-Point Program

Here, as I promised, is a brief summary of the eight-point program for spiritual living which I have been referring to throughout this book. This is the program I myself have followed for almost half a century. Much fuller instructions will be found in my book *Meditation* and in a set of cassettes by the same title.

1. *Meditation.* The heart of this program is meditation: half an hour every morning, as early as is convenient. Instructions will be found on pages 21 – 25; some passages for meditation are listed on page 279.

2. *Repetition of the Holy Name.* This is so simple a practice that it is easy to underestimate its importance. By and large, though it is one of the oldest and most powerful of Christian disciplines, it has survived only in certain monastic traditions. Once you try it, however, I think you will agree that it is also perfectly

adapted to the needs of lay people caught up in the demands of a busy life in the twentieth century. Suggestions for how to use the Holy Name will be found on pages 26 – 29; I have given many more illustrations and applications in my book *The Unstruck Bell*.

3. *Slowing Down.* Hurry makes for tension, insecurity, inefficiency, and superficial living. To guard against hurrying through the day, start the day early and simplify your life so that you do not try to fill your time with more than you can do. When you find yourself beginning to speed up, repeat the Holy Name to help you slow down.

It is important here not to confuse slowness with sloth, which breeds carelessness, procrastination, and general inefficiency. In slowing down we should attend meticulously to details, giving our very best even to the smallest undertaking.

4. *One-pointedness.* Doing more than one thing at a time divides attention and fragments consciousness. When you read and eat at the same time, for example, part of your mind is on what you are reading and part on what you are eating; you are not getting the most from either activity. Similarly, when talking with someone, give that person your full attention. These are little things, but taken together they help to unify consciousness and deepen concentration.

Everything you do should be worthy of your full attention. When the mind is one-pointed it will be secure, free from tension, and capable of the concentration that is the mark of genius in any field.

5. *Training the Senses.* In the food we eat, the books and magazines we read, the movies we see, all of us are subject to the dictatorship of rigid likes and dislikes. To free ourselves from this conditioning, we need to learn to change our likes and dislikes freely when it is in the best interests of those around us or ourselves. We should choose what we eat by what our body needs, for example, rather than by what the taste buds demand.

Similarly, the mind can be said to eat too – through the senses. We need to be very discriminating in what we read and what we go to see for entertainment, for we become in part what our senses take in.

6. *Putting Others First.* Dwelling on ourselves builds a wall between ourselves and others. Those who keep thinking about their needs, their wants, their plans, their ideas cannot help becoming lonely and insecure. The simple but effective technique I recommend is to learn to put other people first – beginning within the circle of your family and friends, where there is already a basis of love on which to build. When husband and wife try to put each other first, for example, they are not only moving closer to each other, they are also removing the barriers of their ego-prison, which deepens their relationships with everyone else as well.

7. *Spiritual Reading.* Our culture is so immersed in what the mass media offer that it is very helpful to balance our outlook by giving half an hour or so each day to spiritual reading – something positive, practical, and inspiring, which reminds us that the spark of divinity is in all of us and can be released in our own lives by meditation, prayer, and daily practice. Just before bedtime is a particularly good time for this kind of reading, because the thoughts you fall asleep in will be with you throughout the night.

8. *Spiritual Association.* When we are trying to change our life, we need the support of others with the same goal. If you have friends who are meditating along the lines suggested here, you can get together regularly to share a meal, meditate, and perhaps read and discuss your spiritual reading. Share your times of entertainment too; relaxation is an important part of spiritual living.

By practicing this eightfold program sincerely and systematically, it is possible for anyone to realize the supreme goal of life. Even a little such practice begins to transform personality, leading to profoundly beneficial changes in ourselves and in the world around us.

Additional Passages for Meditation

To be suitable for meditation, an inspirational passage should come from the scriptures or great mystics and be positive, practical, and personal in its appeal. Here are some of the passages I frequently recommend in addition to those used in this book:

Psalms 22, 23, and 100

The Sermon on the Mount Matthew 5–6 (especially the Beatitudes, Matt. 5:3–16, and the Lord's Prayer, Matt. 6:9–13)

The Wonderful Effect of Divine Love Thomas a Kempis, *Imitation of Christ* I I I . 5

Four Things That Bring Much Inward Peace Thomas a Kempis, *Imitation of Christ* I I I . 23

Lord That Giveth Strength Thomas a Kempis, *Imitation of Christ* I I I . 30

Index

Action: and transformation, 25, 29–34; translating meditation into, 9, 25

addictions: overcoming, 202–203, 204; *see also* habits of mind

anger: evolutionary aspect of, 184–186; and health, 62–63, 185–186, 187; and Holy Name, 33, 170–171, 173; as mask, 129–131; undoing, 185–189

anxiety: avoiding causes of, 154–155; evolutionary aspect of, 189–192; free-floating, 153–154; and health, 62–63; over death, 190–192

Aquinas, Thomas, 141

arrogance: and Paul's epistle on love, 104, 107

attachments, *see* likes and dislikes; personal relationships; selfish desire

attention, one-pointed: defined, 276–277; and energy, 71–72; improving concentration, 197–199; and love, 67–70; and meditation, 67–68, 119; and memory, 119–120, 199–200; and Saul of Tarsus, 81–82; training of, 69–70, 197

Augustine, 254; becomes monk, 138; and Christian mysticism, 140, 141; and *Confessions,* 139, 140–141, 142–143, 144; description of deepest Self, 225–226, 270–271; experience of joy, 231, 233, 234; God as focus of, 231, 253; overview, 136–143; and Roman Catholic Church, 141–142; validation of faith, 235–236, 237, 239; view of mind, 139, 154–155, 160, 181; view of self-will, 160; *see also* Confessions

Bernard of Clairvaux, 8, 141
Bernard of Quintavalle, 27–28

viewing of, 244–245
disease, *see* health
divinity: awareness of, 260–261; evolutionary aspect of, 182–183; seeing in others, 227, 270–271; as universal spark, 139, 260–261; *see also* unity of life

Earth: and human evolution, 178–179; and unity of life, 77; *see also* nations; unity of life
Eckhart, Meister, 203–204, 234
eight-point program, 275–278
energy: conserving, 73–74; and love, 70–74; and negative thoughts, 71–72; rechanneling flow of, 204
eternal life, 267–269
evolution: and anger, 184–186; and anxiety, 189–192; and conditioning, 183–184; and consciousness, 183–184; and divine spark, 182–183; and human mind, 181–182; impact on human personality, 177–189

Faith: validation of, 236–240
forgiveness, 50–51
Fox, George, 8
Francis de Sales, 112
Francis of Assisi: memorials to, 13; overview, 12–19; Prayer of, 19, 20, 21–22, 23, 29–52; seeing attitude of Jesus in, 255; universality of

appeal, 12, 13, 15, 29; validation of faith, 237; writings of, 13, 19, 20; as young man, 14
free-floating thoughts, 118, 153–154
Friars Minor, 14
Friedman, Dr. Meyer, 62, 67, 118
future, 122–123, 135

Gamaliel (rabbi), 81
Gandhi, Mahatma: and power for good, 83, 84; in South Africa, 156; and stress, 150–152, 156
giving, 48–50; *see also* kindness
God, *see* Lord
governments, *see* nations

Habits of mind: Augustine's view of, 139, 160; getting over, 159–164; retraining through meditation, 164, 244–246; tyranny of, 28; *see also* conditioning; desire; likes and dislikes
happiness: Augustine's search for, 136, 140; *see also* joy
health: and anger, 62–63, 185–186, 187; and living habits, 265–267; and need for love, 61–63
heredity, 180; *see also* evolution
Holy Name: basic instruction, 26–28; choice of, 26; and concentration, 115; and consciousness, 27; defined,

Mott, John, 156
Murchie, Guy, 179, 183
mystics: and Christian
  tradition, 140, 141; and consciousness, 178, 183; and
  genius, 221; harnessing negative emotions, 172; inspiration of, 7–8; language of
  love, 252–253; reading
  accounts of, 245; and realization of Lord, 229–231,
  233–235; remaking of
  selves, 248–249

Nations: role of love, 109–110,
  262–264; see also unity of life
negativity: as drain on vital
  energy, 71–72; need to harness emotions, 172–173; see
  also anger; anxiety; resentment
nervous system: as network,
  145–147; response of, 166–
  167; see also health
Nicholas of Cusa, 129

One-pointed attention, see
  attention, one-pointed
Order, see Third Order
other people, see putting
  others first

Paderewski story, 155
pain: making use of, 193–197;
  seeking to escape, 193; sensitivity to, 193–194, 195
pardoning, see forgiveness
patience: and kindness, 102–

104; need for cultivating,
  218–219; and Paul's epistle
  on love, 94–102; practicing
  through meditation, 261–
  262
Paul: "epistle on love," 63,
  86, 87–122; overview,
  80–84
peace, see unity of life; world
  peace
peace of mind, as means to
  larger end, 234–235
Pelé, 76
perfection: vs. imperfection,
  122–129, 131, 132
personal attachments, see likes
  and dislikes; personal relationships; selfish desire
personality: character
  rebuilding, 188–189; impact
  of evolution on, 177–189
personal relationships:
  closeness in, 208–210; and
  concentration, 200–201;
  physical attraction,
  206–207; unselfishness in,
  205–210
planet, see earth
Poor Clares, 14
power for good, 83–84
prayer, see meditation
Prayer of Francis of Assisi, 19,
  20, 21–22, 23, 29–52
Prayer of Quiet, 230–231, 234
putting others first: defined,
  277; difficult people, 35–36,
  166–169, 172–173, 245–246;
  and Francis of Assisi, 18;

getting out of the way, 222–224; vs. having likes and dislikes, 166–171; joy in, 221–223; as opportunity for growth, 172–173; opposing kindly, 167–168

Repression, 10, 241
resentment: and energy, 71–72; and forgiveness, 50–51; heading off, 38; and Holy Name, 118–119, 120, 170–171, 173; and memory, 119–120; and self-will, 117–120
Richard of St. Victor, 141
right desire, *see* selflessness
Rusk, Dean, 187

Sacred passages, *see* inspirational passages
Saul of Tarsus: and one-pointed attention, 81–82; and stoning of Stephen, 82–83; transformation of, 80, 83; *see also* Paul
Schumacher, E.F., 106
scriptures: use in meditation, 23, 24, 25, 188–189, 209, 279
security: and selfless work, 169
Self, real, 124, 269, 273
selfish desire: as drain on vital energy, 72; getting over, 159–164; giving up selfish attachments, 205–210; power of defying, 75–76; vs. right desire, 74–76

selflessness: effect on security, 169; and right desire, 74–76
self-pity: vs. sorrow, 44–45
self-will: extinguishing, 9; getting over, 159–164; and Holy Name, 116; as noise, 9; and Paul's "epistle on love," 110–122; and resentment, 117–120; ridding self of, 30–32
Selye, Dr. Hans, 149, 150
sense pleasures, 251
senses: controlling, 9
sensitivity: to needs of others, 193–197; to pain, 193–194, 195
Sermon on the Mount, 63, 279
Shakespeare, William, 128
shopping: need for one-pointed attention, 198–199; as waste of energy, 73–74
Sisters of Mother Teresa of Calcutta, 54, 55, 57; *see also* Mother Teresa
slowing down, importance of, 276; *see also* mind, quieting
sorrow: vs. self-pity, 44–45
spiritual association, 278
spiritual reading, 278
Steele, Sir Richard, 171
Stephen (Christian martyr), 82–83
stress: and Gandhi, 150–152, 156; and health, 62–63; and likes and dislikes, 149, 167;